The Baggy Green

The text paper used in this book is Monza Satin Recycled. It has 30% pre-consumer and 25% post consumer recycled paper. It has used an ECF (Elemental Chlorine Free) bleaching process and the paper mill is ISO14001 and IPPC endorsed. Monza paper is produced from responsibly managed forests.

THE
BAGGY GREEN

The pride, passion and history of Australia's sporting icon

MICHAEL FAHEY
AND
MIKE COWARD

Craig,

Enjoy the 'Aussie Icon'

Michael Fahey.

FOREWORD BY MARK TAYLOR

Published By
The Cricket Publishing Company
Post Office Box W27
West Pennant Hills
N.S.W. 2125

First Published in March 2008
Reprinted December 2009

The National Library of Australia Cataloguing-in-Publication entry:

Fahey, Michael & Coward, Mike

The Baggy Green: The pride, passion and history of Australia's
sporting icon
1. Cricket – Australia. 2. Cricket players – Australia. 3 Cricket – History

ISBN 0 9775631 1 1

Cover design by Ben Jones

Designed and Typeset by Mercier Typesetters Pty Ltd, Granville NSW in
Stone Serif and Stone Sans Serif

Printed by Ligare Pty Ltd, Riverwood NSW

CONTENTS

ACKNOWLEDGEMENTS

AS soon as I began this project I realised that very little research on the baggy green cap existed and that my frustration was shared by others in auction houses and museums.

I would like to thank the following people:

David Wells at the Bradman Museum in Bowral, who was a cheerful source of much information; Stephen Gibbs, who provided a great treasure of articles and cap references; Cricket Australia's Samantha Burn, Peter Young, Philip Pope and Kelly Sedgeway all provided assistance, as did David Steinhardt, from Velocity Brand Management, who manages licensing for Cricket Australia; Colin Clowes, the librarian at Cricket NSW; Brian Clinton, who painted the *Art of Bradman* portraits; Gideon Haigh, who provided information from the Cricket Australia minutes and who offered learned theories when we were 'stumped' on certain issues.

Journalists Ian Heads and Philip Derriman for their guidance; Richard Cashman and Peter Sharpham for their groundbreaking work on Australian sporting history, especially as the co-authors of the article, 'Symbols, Emblems, Colours and Names'. Roger Page of Roger Page Cricket Books for help in tracking down required publications.

Ross Barrat of Albion C&D, who generously spent a large amount of time providing details about the history of the cap and its manufacture.

Staff at the Melbourne Cricket Club – librarian David Studham and the manager of exhibitions and collections,

Richard Ferguson, who not only discussed the cap, answered questions and provided images, but also contributed a chapter on the museum's collection.

In England I received help from James Greenfield of Yorkshire Cricket Archives; Glenys Williams, MCC archivist and historian at Lord's; Neil Robinson at the MCC Library; Keith Hayhurst from the Old Trafford Museum; Sue Wilson at Lancashire County Cricket Club.

In Australia assistance came from: Cheryl Crilly of the National Museum of Australia; Geoff Havercroft and Steve Hall of the Western Australian Cricket Association; Suzy Russell from the State Library of South Australia and Bernard Whimpress at the South Australian Cricket Association.

Baggy green collectors David Frith (UK), John Kirkness and Harry Wzola.

Max Dunbar of Christies in Britain; Mike Down of Boundary Books; Tom Thompson, who proved auction results for Lawson's and Cromwell's; Charles Leski of Charles Leski Auctions; John Mullock of Mullock's Specialist Auctioneers and Valuers; Michael Treloar Antiquarian Booksellers; Trevor Vennett-Smith from T. Vennett-Smith Auctioneers; David Boxshall of Boxshalls; Graham Budd of Graham Budd Auctions; Tim Knight of Knight's Auctions, David Lee-Steere of Framous Memorabilia Stores; Brett Corrick, general manager/director ISC-Sports; John Fordham of the Fordham Company which manages Mark Taylor; Brenton Siggs, who helped with information regarding the services team; Steve Cashman and the members of the Cricket Memorabilia Society; local collectors and enthusiasts Peter Schofield, Neil Mumford, Rod Mater, Thos Hodgson, and from Zimbabwe Derrick Townsend; Kate Boyd, Ted a'Beckett's daughter.

I am grateful for the time Guy Masters and Katie Fahey spent reading the manuscript.

Rod Parkes from Getty Images provided photographs. Ben Jones at Legends did a wonderful job creating the front and back covers; Victor Yoog, my partner at Legends, gave his support and guidance.

Our editor, Mark Ray, provided a unique pool of literary, photographic and cricketing experience. My co-author Mike Coward brought a wealth of cricket knowledge, sober judgement and wise counsel.

Finally, calling Ronald Cardwell a cricket publisher is like calling Rupert Murdoch a paper-seller. Ronald's skill in presenting the world of cricket folklore and previously unknown facts to the mainstream through his publications, lectures and dinners is amazing.

Michael Fahey
March 2008

ii

FOREWORD

T HE baggy green cap is a powerful and timeless symbol which connects Victor Trumper to Ricky Ponting.

A cricket cap is much more than part of a uniform. I have all my caps from the time I started playing in a team and each one evokes precious memories of people, matches and moments. In a sense they are an archive.

Being awarded a baggy green is the ultimate for a cricketer in Australia and I am proud to have ensured the significance of this badge of honour is appreciated by everyone who loves the game in Australia and abroad.

Before a Test match in 1994 it was decided that each member of the Australian team should wear the cap in the first fielding session of a Test match. The intention was to show off the beauty of the cap and our pride in it; not to intimidate our opponents. But there is no doubt that its aura provides Australian teams with a psychological edge.

There was never any intention to commercialise the cap or to imply that the contemporary cricketer placed more importance upon it than his predecessors.

The baggy green is revered by everyone with a connection to Australian cricket, and this rich and revealing account of its history and rise to prominence is timely. It will be enthusiastically welcomed by those privileged to have worn the cap and, no doubt, by all those who dreamed of doing so.

Every cricketer to have represented Australia has made a priceless contribution to the history of the game. They are a disparate group of characters who have served through good and bad times over 130 years and are bound together because they have worn with distinction the baggy green cap or its antecendent.

More power to them and may they long be recognised for their contribution to Australia's sporting and social history.

Mark Taylor
Sydney, March 2008

Honoured role ... Mark Taylor, the 39th Test captain of Australia.
Photo: Getty Images

1
THE PRIDE OF THE BAGGY GREEN

CRICKET occupies a unique place in Australian sport. It was the first national game and remains so after more than a hundred years. It is a game whose national side significantly predates the Australian teams of all other major codes and even the Federation of the Australian colonies. Given this long pre-eminence, it is unusual that the national cricket team has not had either a name or a logo marketed, especially in this more brand-conscious era.

On the cricket field the only item of uniform that clearly identifies one side from another is the cap. The Australian Test cap is colloquially called the 'baggy green', and recently this term has sometimes been applied to the team and to cricket in Australia in general.

Not registered until recently by Australian cricket administrators, the term has come to be used by various commercial and non-commercial organisations. Baggygreen. com, operated by Nine MSN, is the name of Cricinfo's Australian website. Also there is a cricket journal – *The Baggy Green* – which is produced independently of Cricket Australia.

The Australian cap's nickname has, therefore, come to be the name of cricket as a game and as a commercial activity in Australia. However little is known about the cap's origins. Many, for instance, still believe the coat of arms on the cap is that of the Australian government – the official national coat of arms. This is not the case. Even the Australian government's website, 'Australia Now', erroneously states: 'The Australian Government uses the coat of arms to authenticate documents and for other official purposes. Its uses range from embellishing the Australian passport to being widely recognised as the badge on the famous "baggy green" cricket cap.'[1]

Such misapprehensions have been accepted widely. The coat of arms on the Test cap predates Federation and the subsequent development of the official national coat of arms.

Although there has been no official marketing campaign, the extensive use of the name 'baggy green' and the wider appreciation of the cap have grown dramatically in the past 10 years. Steve Waugh's attachment to his dilapidated cap is widely known. This increased the appreciation of the cap as an icon that represents cricket at all levels while at the same time remaining a membership badge to a select club – Australian Test representatives, of which at the time of writing there were just 399 members.

So renowned was the baggy green that in 2003 when Roger Knight, in his role as the Marylebone Cricket Club's (MCC) chief executive, announced[2] a new relationship between the club and Albion, the maker of the baggy green cap, he said: 'We are delighted to be joining forces with a company of Albion's calibre. Its baggy green is the most famous cricket cap in the world.'[3]

Many people believe that the cap is so sacred an icon that it has never changed over the years. Again, this is not so; there have been many changes.

The unravelling of the cap's history and its personal significance to players, public and collectors will help explain why the baggy green has been elevated to such a position of sporting and social esteem.

The recent rise in the cap's profile is a three-fold story.

First, this rise has been led by the players. Recent Test captains – Allan Border, Mark Taylor and Steve Waugh –

understood the cap's powerful symbolism to current players and instituted a number of ceremonies and conventions designed to reinforce the cap's special place in the culture of the game.

Second, market forces have demanded the creation of brands and the Australian Cricket Board and the renamed Cricket Australia embraced this with the creation of logos on shirts and sunhats. Throughout this process the administrators were determined not to commercialise the baggy green and to retain the original badge on the cap.

Third, the development of a commercial memorabilia market has increased the prestige of the baggy green cap. In Australia this market did not exist before 1993 but the marketing on the Nine Network of licensed products helped establish a revenue stream for the players, their association (Australian Cricketers' Association) and the sport's governing

On top down under ... nowadays the baggy green takes pride of place in the kit of the Australian cricketer. **Photo: Mark Ray**

body (Cricket Australia). As well, the growth of the market for memorabilia meant that the exclusive group of serious collectors was exposed to a wider collecting market.

People have been selling or swapping cricketania for more than 100 years. However for most of that time the market was based in England and required substantial research and good connections. New Australian money entered the English cricket memorabilia market in the late 1980s[4]. The success of Australian teams since the 1987 World Cup win and the 1989 Ashes victory meant that the market became global; the old system became obsolete. Higher prices and greater demand meant that the market expanded and the extra exposure meant that more items were valued rather than discarded or simply forgotten.

Later in these pages we will examine the reactions of former and current Australian players to the current iconic status of the baggy green cap. We will also explore the media hype and high prices surrounding various Bradman cap auctions and acquisitions, and how these developments fit into the history of the baggy green cap.

MF

References

1 http://www.dfat.gov.au/facts/coat_of_arms.html.
2 MCC press release, 22/9/2003.
3 Lord's press release 22/9/2003.
4 *The Wisden Book of Cricket Memorabilia*, Lennard Publishing 1990. Appendix, page 315: 'The aggressive bidding of the Antipodeans was enjoyed by all at the MCC Bicentenary auction, glowering away at each other.'

2
CAPTIVATED

THE romanticising of the baggy green was so pervasive by October 2004 that Michael Clarke discarded his helmet and called for his brand new cap as he drew within two runs of a priceless century in his first Test innings.

For a 23-year-old greenhorn with a rudimentary knowledge of his illustrious predecessors and the game's history it was a powerful and symbolic act which soon became a part of the rich lore of Australian cricket.

An irrepressible young man with an endearing if roguish smile, Clarke reasoned that it would be tantamount to irreverence to realise his greatest dream wearing a helmet and not the iconic baggy green.

From the time he entered the first-class arena with New South Wales at the age of 18 and his dreams of Test selection intensified he promised himself and those closest to him that should he ever get the chance to score a hundred for Australia it would be achieved under the baggy green.

When the moment came he kissed the cap and cried tears of happiness.

'I would like to have held on to that moment for longer; to remember what that feeling was like,' Clarke said.

But he was consumed by emotions of such intensity that he was numbed. To this day he has no recollection of who brought the cap to him in the middle and what, if anything, was said.

He remembers it was presented to him before the match by Shane Warne but guiltily confesses to not remembering a word his good friend said in commendation and congratulation. Such was his trance-like state, he simply stared at the cap through tears. His moment, the one of which he had dared to dream since his childhood, was upon him. A baggy green was his.

While a raised and kissed helmet has become an increasingly familiar response to the acclaim of crowds since the late 1970s it is the doffing of the cap which maintains tradition and so evokes memories of the greatest batsmen and their finest deeds.

By holding aloft his cap Clarke also effectively paid homage to the 11 other Australians who announced their brilliance with a hundred in their first Test innings – a disparate band headed by Charles Bannerman who amassed an undefeated 165 in the first Test in March 1877.

While Bannerman wore a cap of a different style and colour the legendary quartet of Bill Ponsford, Archie Jackson, Doug Walters and Greg Chappell accomplished the feat in the name of the baggy green during a 45-year period – before the helmet became de rigueur.

The baggy green cap has become a centrepiece of Australia's vibrant cricket history. It is the one constant; a reassuring reference point in a game which is forever changing and has done so at disconcerting speed since the World Series Cricket schism of 1977-79.

However, the modern masters are proud of being imbued with the spirit of the past and Clarke's triumph effectively linked the events at the M. Chinnaswamy Stadium in Bangalore, the garden city of India, in 2004 with the first Test at Melbourne, in the garden state of Victoria, 127 years earlier.

That this connection was highlighted in the media gladdened the hearts of Mark Taylor and Steve Waugh,

At the helm ... Steve Waugh strikes an authoritative pose at the toss, First Test, Kandy, Sri Lanka in 1999. The next day he was as battered as his fabled cap after a sickening collision with Jason Gillespie. **Photo: Mark Ray**

Australia's Test match captains from September 1994 to January 2004, and justified their earnest endeavours to ensure the first elite cricketers of the 21st century were aware of the identity and deeds of those who had gone before them.

Taylor, renowned for his calm control and tactical acumen, felt strongly that more attention needed to be paid to the significance of the cap and that greater efforts be made to distinguish it from the flotsam and jetsam associated with the modern game.

When he began his Test career against the West Indies in 1988-89 Taylor received his baggy green in a metre-square cardboard box. At least the cap was on top of the training shirts and jumpers. Four years earlier Dean Jones opened the package sent to the family home at Mount Waverley in Victoria and needed to dig deep through shirts and jumpers to find his precious cap at the bottom of the pile.

Bob Merriman, a distinguished administrator who managed Australian teams to India, England, New Zealand and Sharjah in the United Arab Emirates in the 1970s and 1980s before rising to be chairman of Cricket Australia, vividly recalls then Australian Cricket Board secretary Alan Barnes distributing caps to Kim Hughes's team to India in 1979 as though he was delivering newspapers from a moving vehicle. The caps were tossed across a room.

Such an absence of ceremony disappointed Taylor who had fond memories of the ritual guernsey presentation nights at his Tigers Australian football club at Wagga Wagga in his youth.

Two years after succeeding Allan Border as captain and insisting each member of the team wear the baggy green cap for the first session of the first Test match with England at the Gabba in November 1994, Taylor instituted a formal cap presentation.

Before the first Test with the West Indies in Brisbane in November 1996 he called his men together and chose his words carefully as he presented caps to Michael Kasprowicz and Matthew Elliott.

For Kasprowicz, a genial, lion-hearted pace bowler who gave yeoman service for the next decade, the formal presentation of the cap brought another unforgettable dimension to his debut before his home crowd.

'The celebration of the cap is a good idea – it is something special because the game is so rich and steeped in history,' said Kasprowicz.

'In these changing times of Twenty-20, graphite strips on bats and different rules changes the baggy green represents constancy. It is a constant and that's the beauty of it.

'The cap is a special part of you – almost like a tattoo. You only realise the power of it when you are in and out of the team. I always try and capture the moment in case it is the last time I play or share the dressingroom. I never take it for granted.'

Kasprowicz's analogous use of 'tattoo' is appropriate. Among his peers Colin Miller marked his brief but fascinating 18-match 'mid-life' Test career with an image of the baggy green tattooed on a buttock. Michael Slater, Mark Waugh, Michael Clarke and Ricky Ponting have had their Test cap number tattooed on various parts of their body – Clarke's 389 boldly in Roman numerals across the small of his back.

'You only scar your body for something precious,' he said.

Steve Waugh brought another dimension to subsequent cap presentation ceremonies after he took over the captaincy in the West Indies in 1999. To mark the induction of Adam Gilchrist and Scott Muller into the team for the first Test with Pakistan in the summer of 1999-2000 he called upon the late Bill Brown to present their caps and so welcome them into the family of Australian Test cricketers. Brown, a former Australian captain and a member of Don Bradman's legendary Invincibles in England in 1948, said he was immensely proud to be involved in such a presentation 65 years after receiving his first baggy green to very little fanfare at Nottingham in England.

Bill Brown died, aged 95, in March 2008. Steve Waugh told the *Courier-Mail*: 'I reckon that if one person could have their picture beside the baggy green cap to illustrate what it stood for, it should be Bill. Bill was the man who my generation really looked up to. For us he was the embodiment of everything great about the baggy green cap. He had everything – strength, great ethics, character and wonderful stories from the past and yet still had great respect for the modern game.'

Inseparable ... opening batting partners Bill Brown, resplendent in his baggy green cap, and Jack Fingleton in light-hearted mood as they head for a spot of tennis during the 1938 tour of England. **Photo: courtesy Ronald Cardwell**

This affable soul so beloved by Australia's contemporary players was bemused at the importance placed upon the cap and the commercial value ascribed to it since the early 1990s.

'In my day they were just cricket caps and flung into our bags,' Brown said in late 2007. 'They were just part of the attire and not regarded much higher than your boots and treated much the same. We didn't look after them. Undoubtedly if I had my time over again I would treat them with greater care. I'm sorry now. But it was my fault,' added Brown, who did not have a cap in his collection of memorabilia at his Brisbane home.

Like so many players down the years he gave his caps away and smiled at the recollection of a grandchild wearing one of his baggy greens to a Sunday school picnic.

Throughout his phenomenal career Gilchrist felt a special bond with the indefatigable Brown and always looked forward to meeting him on the cricket circuit.

That the baggy green is now widely seen as embodying the spirit and history of Australian cricket and not merely as part of the playing uniform is one of the greatest legacies of the mightily successful Taylor-Waugh era.

Allan Border, who so gallantly constructed the platform from which Taylor and Waugh continued to advance Australia fair, fervently believes the rest of the cricket world is deeply jealous of the awesome power the cap engenders.

'I think it is fantastic that the baggy green has this iconic status,' said Border. 'The aura and historical significance of the cap gives Australian teams a psychological advantage. Other teams may be proud of their cap but don't talk about it with the same passion.

'By all wearing the cap in the first session it has an aura and the team is making a statement. Steve Waugh deserves much credit for initiating or rekindling the spirit of the baggy green. He has given it great focus. It is a tremendous legacy.'

Waugh, whose voice was said to be loudest at the memorable team meeting in Brisbane in 1994 which led to all 11 players wearing the baggy green in the first session, played on for five years after Taylor retired at the age of 34 at the end of the 1998-99 international summer. By the time he bade an emotional farewell against India in the first week of January 2004, Waugh was within six months of his 39th birthday and any image of him without his beloved if battered baggy green seemed incomplete and inappropriate. Waugh and his cap were inseparable as the Australian people rose to him.

Waugh's deep affection for the traditional game and its lustrous history and timeless values and virtues never blunted his enthusiasm for the frenetic and often crudely played and marketed limited-overs game.

Together with thrilling extrovert batsman Dean Jones he was an unabashed fan and promoter of compressed cricket, and it was his phenomenal all-round exploits at the 1987 World Cup on the Indian sub-continent which largely forged his cricket persona and earned him the sobriquet of 'iceman'.

When the Australian selectors controversially decided to differentiate between five-day and one-day cricket for the summer of 1997-98 Waugh was appointed captain for limited-overs matches and Taylor remained at the helm in Test matches.

While the one-day game has enormous appeal to spectators, especially women, adolescents and children, it is considered an amusing and lucrative distraction by the vast majority of elite players who judge their peers on their ability in the traditional arena. Critics, too, hold a similar view.

While he was as anxious as Taylor to lift the profile of the baggy green and draw public attention to the significance of a player's designated place in his history of the game, Waugh was concerned that specialist one-day players could be overlooked by contemporaries, commentators and, indeed, by history.

It was this concern which prompted him to suggest that the Australian one-day squad wear their allocated numbers on their coloured caps during the triumphant 1999 World Cup campaign in England and Wales.

He felt strongly that it would provide the team with a sense of belonging. It was not, however, an initiative that could be acted upon at a moment's notice after an often fraught, drawn Test series in the West Indies.

Ever the lateral thinker, Waugh sought the help and local knowledge of his genial all-rounder and one-day specialist Tom Moody, who continued to win impressive notices for his leadership of Worcestershire in English county cricket.

Before the opening match against Scotland at the picturesque Worcester ground Waugh and Moody thumbed through the yellow pages of regional telephone directories and eventually reached an affable grandmother who assured them she could produce the numbers required for embroidering onto the two caps of each of the 15 Australian players. It was as well she lived in Cardiff where Australia was to play New Zealand in their second match. In the end the senior seamstress' work, completed in just two days, was a little too bold and Waugh opted for an alternative.

It was from this initiative by Waugh that England's Test players wore their designated number on their shirts for the Ashes series of 2001, and Waugh ensured that the Australians followed suit against New Zealand and South Africa in 2001-02.

While Waugh's cap is among the most venerated items of Australian cricketania it is not the only baggy green Waugh donned in his remarkable career. Nor is it clear if it is the cap presented on his debut against India at Melbourne in December 1985. Waugh had long believed – and, indeed, recorded in his autobiography – that his celebrated cap was the first he ever received as a member of the Australian Under-19 team which played Pakistan in 1984. This team, which also included his twin brother Mark and Mark Taylor, was indeed furnished with baggy greens but they were emblazoned with 'Youth XI'.

Furthermore he played in another cap in England in 1993, having misplaced, temporarily as it happened, the cap in use in the summer of 1992-93. So he played in at least two and in all probability, three caps which is scarcely surprising given that his Test career spanned a tad over 18 years.

Conversely, Taylor, who often favoured a white floppy hat because of fears he was susceptible to skin cancers, is convinced he used just one baggy green throughout his 10-year, 104-Test career. That he has two others in pristine condition bespeaks the generosity of spirit of Lawrie Sawle, one of the great servants of Australian cricket, who managed Taylor's triumphant party to the Caribbean in 1995. Justin Langer is, perhaps, the only other long-serving player of this spectacularly successful period who can lay claim to using just the one cap for more than 100 Test matches. And he quipped at his valedictory press conference at the close of the 2006-07 Ashes series that its stench was such that it would need to be housed behind thick glass. Certainly, at least David Boon, Adam Gilchrist and Ricky Ponting, for one reason or another, used two caps.

Ponting, the 42nd Australian captain, was inspired by the philosophy of Waugh and Taylor – under whom he made his Test debut as a 20-year-old in 1995 – and as he grew in confidence at the helm was keen to maintain and, indeed, build on the traditions. Very much his own man he wasted little time in discarding the garish striped team blazers which to his dismay had been favoured for a period.

As far as he was concerned these had no connection to the traditions of Australian cricket. He had them replaced with a striking green blazer with gold piping fashioned after that worn by Don Bradman during his period as captain from 1936 to 1948.

As intent as his immediate predecessors to make a lasting contribution to the livery of the Australian team, Ponting had 42 embroidered into the pocket of the blazer. And at the start of the 2007-08 season he was pondering the wisdom of introducing specific caps to identify the captain and those privileged to have played in 100 or more Test matches.

Ponting has never worn anything other than the baggy green and with the emphatic support of his deputy Adam Gilchrist urges all players to wear it at all times. Those reluctant to conform – Shane Warne and Mark Waugh were cases in point – were regularly if gently taunted by the leadership group. Ponting makes no apology for this. Indeed, he also likes his men to wear the cap at the start of a fielding session. And it must be worn at victory celebrations which culminate with the intoning of the team anthem. At Ponting's direction such flannelled corroborees have taken place atop Table Mountain at Cape Town in South Africa and at the spectacular 17th century Galle Fort in Sri Lanka.

At these intimate gatherings sponsors' caps are removed and the baggy green worn. This ritual seems to have had its genesis at Manchester when Allan Border's team so famously regained the Ashes in 1989. After the initial champagne and beer swilling and spraying celebration in the dressingroom David Boon and his close pal Geoff Marsh walked to their kitbags and put on their caps. It was unrehearsed and further stirred emotions in the dressingroom. It just seemed the right thing to do.

Ponting, like Taylor and Waugh before him, believes the uniform wearing of the baggy green in the first session of a Test match is a compelling aesthetic which provides the Australians with an aura and thus a competitive edge. And he makes certain his younger charges, Michael Clarke in particular, are cognisant of their responsibilities to the baggy green and to the exclusive band of men who have worn it.

'I have the ultimate respect for the cap and if I have any input into the next generation I will see the tradition continues,' declared Clarke.

Vivid memories of the awesome 1980s West Indians, men who seemed as tall, strong and immovable as the palm tree on their caps, prompted Waugh to discuss the matter at the team meeting in Brisbane in 1994. He felt strongly that along with the swagger the cap had provided the West Indians with a unity of purpose and an air of invincibility. It was something he wanted the Australians to emulate.

However, as far as skipper Taylor was concerned the decision for all 11 players to wear the cap onto the Gabba at the start of the Ashes series was made in the name of aesthetics.

'It was not designed to scare the opposition. It was designed to look good for the side,' said Taylor.

Whether such regimentation has ever unsettled opponents is debatable. Richie Benaud is sure Don Bradman once told him he had used the ploy in England in 1948 but this could not be corroborated by Sam Loxton and Arthur Morris, members of Bradman's Invincibles.

The baggy green elicits a multiplicity of emotions and attitudes from those privileged to have worn it. Without exception these men, famous and forgotten, speak of a profound sense of pride and privilege. Some talk of the humbling nature of attaining it, others of an awesome responsibility to justify selection and to serve the ghosts of summers long gone. There are those who speak unselfconsciously of a reverence for the cap and those who foresee dangers in its worship. Some, former captain Bob Simpson among them, contend it should be worn only in pristine condition and abhor the contemporary practice of wearing the cap to the point of disintegration. Utter nonsense counter others who have guarded their cap with their sporting life.

While the intrinsic value of the baggy green has always been appreciated, its commercial worth and desirability to collectors and investors is a consequence of the cap culture developed by Taylor and Waugh.

Indeed, Simpson and fast bowler Frank Misson are among those who attest to the fact that in the 1950s and 1960s the baggy green was never referred to as such. It was a cap and nothing more than a cap; an item of apparel in their kit. And that is where it generally stayed between matches. It was respected, for it had long been coveted, but it was never idolised.

'In 1961 there was not the depth of emotion associated with the cap,' said Misson. 'It was referred to as the "cap" and not the "baggy green" and if anything, there was more emphasis on the romance of the colours of green and gold. There was probably a feeling that the cap was a little unfashionable. Most other countries had a baseball or skull cap. Certainly ours was more flouncy. I think there was a thought it was a bit old-fashioned and the other countries looked a little more sartorial.'

As rumbustious fast bowler Jeff Thomson observed with customary succinctness: 'The main thing was to be in the team. It had nothing to do with the cap. Even if I had nothing I'd know I'd played for Australia.' Bill Lawry concurred: 'The cap was nice but it was the honour of playing that meant most, be it for club, state or country.'

By the time Waugh had retired in 2004 Taylor recognised that the new culture of the baggy green and the inevitable media and auction house emphasis on its steadily increasing dollar value had polarised a good number of former Australian players.

'My intention was never to commercialise the baggy green,' said Taylor. 'It disappoints me a little that it has become a commercial item rather than a personal one. I would hate to think that players would look to it as an investment. I'm sure this is not the case.

'I am concerned that it might seem to make the players of today more valuable than the players of the past. That is certainly not the case. I wanted to make the cap something special and keep it apart from the paraphernalia. There is just so much stuff that I didn't want the baggy green to get lost. That I have played a small part in making the baggy green such a strong and recognisable national symbol makes me very proud.'

Many of Taylor's predecessors are among those with the greatest reservations about the wider community's fascination with the baggy green and the monetary value now attached to it.

'I say this not in a derogatory way but it has only been in recent times there has been this kerfuffle about the baggy green,' said Richie Benaud. 'There used not to be anyone beating their breast or talking about the baggy green. And no one was spraying beer over it. I was proud of playing for Australia and I don't feel any different about the Australian cap as I did when I was playing and captain. It is a piece of memorabilia and I've never been a memorabilia person.'

Indeed, other than photographs of a special gathering of Australian captains in Brisbane, Allan Border's triumphant Australians at Old Trafford in 1989 and a splendid image of the Sydney Cricket Ground in 1880 given to him by Ian and Barbara Chappell, Benaud has little cricket memorabilia at his home at the beachside suburb of Coogee in Sydney.

Benaud has long dined out on the fact that one of his baggy green caps bought for 50 cents at an opportunity shop at Dee Why on Sydney's northern beaches sold for $10,925 the day a Bradman bat fetched $32,200 at auction.

While he wore his cap in his first Test against the West Indies in January 1952 and for much of the following summer against South Africa, for the rest of his distinguished 63-Test career to February 1964 he was, much like his faithful deputy, Neil Harvey, mostly bare-headed in the middle whether batting or fielding.

Lawry, who made his Test debut under Benaud in 1961 and was destined to succeed Bob Simpson as captain in 1967, simply noted: 'These are different times and there is now a commercial value rather than a sentimental value attached to the baggy green.'

However, it is Ian Chappell who followed Lawry at the helm in February 1971 who is characteristically strident.

'There's only one way you get a slouch hat and one way you get a baggy green. You play or you fought,' said Chappell. 'And I would never wear a slouch hat because I never fought.

'A lot of what goes on with the baggy green is for commercial reasons and I have a major problem with that,' said Chappell who, like Benaud, does not possess a baggy green cap other than the miniature that was presented along with a plaque declaring each player's designated place in batting order since March 15, 1877. Chappelli is number 231.

'Playing for Australia was really important. Not the cap. I don't ever remember having one discussion about the cap during my playing days.'

Nor can Chappell recall his famous grandfather, Vic Richardson, ever playfully placing a baggy green on his head as he netted with brothers Greg and Trevor in the backyard of the family home at North Glenelg in Adelaide.

Richardson, who played 19 Test matches and led Australia to a spectacular 4-0 success against South Africa in 1935-36, never drew attention to his accomplishments and kept his baggy green at the bottom of the canvas bag which had found its way to the Chappell household. The boys were much more interested in the bats, balls and baseball gloves with which they could play.

While he was proud to have earned his baggy green Chappell considered it only another item of apparel and, much like his grandfather, disliked ostentatious displays of the cap.

Widely acknowledged as one of the game's most inspirational leaders, Chappell's forthright if not bolshie approach to aspects of the captaincy alienated the game's conservative governors with whom he was often in conflict.

He captained Australia throughout the 1970s to a backcloth of social restlessness and non-conformity, and the casualness in dress – floppy white hats were in vogue – and demeanour of his men earned them the unwanted label of the 'Ugly Australians'. Be that as it may, they were much loved by the Australian people, and nearly 40 years later the leading lights of the Chappell era still occupy a special place in the hearts and minds of the Australian cricket community.

That the baggy green was not uniformly worn through this period was interpreted by many as an anti-establishment gesture by Chappell and the revolutionaries at his command. To a man they were tired of being treated as serfs by the masters in mahogany row at the then Australian Cricket Board and sought drastic changes to every aspect of the game. By 1977 the winds of change had gathered cyclonic velocity.

So pervasive was the anti-establishment sentiment that John Inverarity, who toured England in 1968 and 1972 and for a short time was deputy to Chappell, felt out of place if he wore cap and blazer. Kim Hughes, who was destined to captain his country, experienced similar feelings of alienation.

'At Arundel (for the traditional one-day Ashes tour opener) I put my cap on because it was an opportunity to do so,' said Inverarity. 'Then I realised I was the only who was capped and so proud to be so. At the same time I was aware that such an expression of this pride was infra dig. I felt a little self-conscious but felt I wasn't in a position to share that thought for it was a little too earnest or conscientious.'

Hughes, 10 years younger than Inverarity, a fellow West Australian, felt that the cap and blazer were neither worn nor respected when he entered the international arena at the very time the startling details of the World Series Cricket upheaval were reaching the public domain.

'I wanted to sleep in my cap, I was so excited,' observed Hughes, who at 23 was chosen for the final Test in England in 1977 under the captaincy of Greg Chappell. 'I had worked so hard for it, so had my parents and my coach. And it wasn't required. I found that awkward but it was the times – the time of anti-establishment feelings.'

Greg Chappell's view of the baggy green was starkly different to his older brother's and in 2007-08 he kept one in storage as he flitted about the world meeting commercial commitments which arose primarily as a result of his tumultuous two-year stint as coach of the Indian cricket team.

'The cap was always important to me but not in the way it has become today,' said Greg Chappell. 'It was always something special to pull it on and I was always aware of the history and what had gone before. It might not have been the focus of so much as it is today but it was certainly a powerful symbol.'

Doug Walters, one of Ian Chappell's closest mates, concedes he often reflects on the aberration of predominantly wearing the white floppy hat.

'I didn't wear the cap much at all. We wore the white floppies. I don't know why, really. It was a stupid trend. Why would you wear the floppy when you could wear the cap?' asked Walters almost plaintively.

'The baggy green was something I dreamed of getting as a kid. I knew that was the ultimate and I told my school teachers I didn't have to do homework because I would play Test cricket for Australia and wear the baggy green. They dismissed such a notion but I proved them wrong.'

A renowned raconteur, Walters donated the bulk of his caps to various charitable causes over many years but cherishes his first baggy presented before he became just the fifth Australian to score a century in his first Test innings – a glorious 155 against England at Brisbane in December 1965.

That more than 25 years after his retirement from Test cricket Walters laments not wearing his cap more often is indicative of the renewed respect afforded the baggy green since Taylor and Waugh devised means to add to its lustre.

Indeed, respect for the cap and its lustre in the most literal sense, is an issue which polarises those who have served the baggy green. Steve Waugh, in particular, was widely criticised, indeed, condemned in some quarters for wearing his famous cap in such a decrepit state. His contemporaries, most notably Justin Langer, defended him vigorously, but seeing a dilapidated baggy green publicly paraded has irritated a host of former players.

Geoff Lawson, who played alongside Waugh in 10 Test matches between November 1986 and December 1989, was most annoyed.

'I certainly have not liked the fact that Steve Waugh wore his baggy green until it had fallen apart,' Lawson said. 'I thought that disrespectful. It looked tatty and neglectful. I'm not quite sure what his aim was. But it was disrespectful not respectful.'

Keith Stackpole, who played 43 times for Australia and for a period was vice-captain to Ian Chappell, has been well known for his strident observations as a radio and newspaper critic since he retired from the first-class arena in 1973-74.

'I see faded caps, caps out of shape, and I don't like it,' observed Stackpole. 'Caps are meant to be worn in pristine condition.

'I don't go along with all this nonsense about the baggy green cap. I don't like the way it has gone. It's purely commercial and has gone over the top. We used to have a fitting for the cap – now there is elastic on the side. I think the cap would have meant more in the old days when they batted in them. I can't understand why they mean that much when they don't bat in the things. In the old days players would practise in them too. But not now.'

Stackpole and the baggy green were not a natural fit. While his heart swelled with pride at the honour of representing his country he found the plastic in the centre of the cap lining caused him to sweat profusely. He even pondered whether the constant and intense sweating contributed to the melanoma on his scalp which he had to battle later in life. Coincidentally, his protégé, Dean Jones, complained that the cap constantly gave him headaches.

Colin McDonald and Bob Simpson, who opened the batting in four of the five Tests of the epic series with the West Indies in 1960-61, expressed concerns at trends in the contemporary game.

McDonald, who played 47 Tests between 1952 and 1961 (14 with Simpson) recalled that 'baggy green' was a part of the game's lexicon when he began his Test career in 1952.

'I'm all for the fact it has such status now, that it is an iconic item of memorabilia,' said McDonald. 'I'm pleased it has this status and that the current players value it so highly. But I was disappointed when Steve Waugh and others wore the cap in such a dilapidated state. It was a shame he did that. I don't think he realised how dreadful it looked. Perhaps Cricket Australia should set down a rule that they have to be changed periodically to guard against dilapidation. It is important to maintain the look and image of such a prestigious item.

'I'm disappointed in the way the cap looks nowadays. It has been denigrated a bit and looks bad on the modern player,' said Simpson. 'Wearing them for so long probably has come about because of superstition. But it suggests a lack of respect. Be assured the cap earned great respect and it made a big difference overseas and was talked about because it was so different from the others. But to make a full impact and be seen at its best it must be in pristine condition. It was unsaid but understood that the cap was to be worn in pristine condition.'

Ross Edwards, a gritty middle-order batsman and glorious cover fieldsman in 20 Tests in the 1970s, believes that superstition will have wittingly or unwittingly contributed to the fashion of wearing the cap to the point of its disintegration.

'It has partly to do with the fact that cricketers are superstitious,' said Edwards. 'If you get runs in a cap you wear it. I'm not sure whether you should tour with a crappy old cap. That's the individual's choice. I couldn't do that. But if you had a cap and you weren't getting runs in it, it would be a temptation to go back to the one from the past.'

Justin Langer, the most loyal of Steve Waugh's acolytes, was irritated beyond measure at the carping directed at his guru for wearing a badly frayed baggy green. In his book *The Power of Passion*, Langer wrote: 'As far as I am concerned these people mustn't have anything better to talk about. Like the martial arts master, Steve Waugh's cap is symbolic of everything that is great about Steve Waugh and Australian cricket.'

In recent years 'baggy green' has found its way into the index to the memoirs of some contemporary players. This is a far cry from the reference to the sub-heading of 'Cap' under 'Equipment' in Don Bradman's famous text of 1958, *The Art of Cricket*. He wrote: 'Unless the weather is dull, I think it advisable to wear a cap. I have seen more than one player affected by the sun in hot climates and I have also seen many catches missed by capless players who would certainly have had a better chance of seeing the ball with a cap on.'

Brian Booth, an admired Christian gentleman, mentor and educationist who represented Australia at both hockey and cricket, has deep respect for the baggy green but warns against its glorification.

'The commercialisation of the caps doesn't faze me but I am uneasy about the idol worship. I certainly don't bow down to them,' said Booth who twice deputised for his injured and ill skipper Bob Simpson during the 1965-66 Ashes series.

Jeff Thomson is of like mind. 'Of course it means something to get one but I'm not one to sit around and kiss the cap and blazer,' he said. 'Anyway, they didn't have the value when I was playing. They could be replaced and were often swapped.'

His great pal Len Pascoe found a baggy green lying in the dressingroom at the end of a day's play at Lord's in 1977. None of his teammates ever claimed it.

Such is the modern aura of the baggy green that initially it can overwhelm, even intimidate, the recipient.

'I can recall when I first received the cap sitting in my room and holding it and wondering whether I was worthy of it,' said David Boon. 'The cap is the tangible representation of the privilege of playing for Australia. Everything is represented by the cap. I valued it more as my career unfolded and you keep it on your head for as long as you can. And when you no longer wear it, it is sacred.'

Pascoe vividly remembers being consumed by self-doubt as Greg Chappell's Ashes party winged its way to England in 1977.

'I confessed to Max Walker that I just didn't know if I was good enough,' Pascoe said. 'Max told me that when I had the baggy green on my head I would be the best my country would offer and I would play as it was meant to be.

'He said: "You will have a sense of security, you will have the history of the cap and its traditions and it will give you the confidence to be the best you can be. This is the essence of the baggy green."'

Pascoe played 14 Test matches and had the distinction of sharing the attack with Thomson, the incomparable Dennis Lillee as well as his guide Walker. Indeed, he shared the new ball with Lillee in the Centenary Test at Lord's in 1980.

That legendary bowler and critic Bill O'Reilly had told Pascoe's father to remind his son he was not playing just for himself but for the ghosts of the past had only served to heighten Pascoe's nervousness.

To a man the cricket community understood that O'Reilly did not mince words and in the 1960s had famously and loudly told his down-and-out teammate 'Chuck' Fleetwood-Smith to never again sully the baggy green by wearing it when drinking with his hobo mates beneath the Princes Bridge in Melbourne.

'Players recognise the sense of humility that comes with the cap and with wearing the cap,' said Pascoe.

How Rodney Hogg, another forthright paceman of the period, would have enjoyed having Pascoe and company at his side. But the fair, green-eyed tearaway was pressed into service under Graham Yallop's leadership against England in 1978-79 at the height of the World Series Cricket upheaval and essentially had to fend for himself and carry the attack.

'I went into an Australian side so raw there was no one really to impart the traditions of the baggy green,' said Hogg, whose Test career prospered for the next six years and earned him 123 wickets.

These days there is not an elite player in the country who does not know the traditions of the baggy green. And, given the chance, each will impart that legacy to those chosen to follow in their stead.

MC

— CAPITAL APPRECIATION —

Since the mid-1990s intense public interest in the cultural and monetary significance of the baggy green has caused cap owners to experience a full range of emotions.

Certainly there are a good number of Test cricketers and their descendants who regret they were so unsentimental about the cap. Baggy greens have been lost, sold, swapped, given, loaned, donated and neglected. Arthur Morris and Neil Harvey, two of the four surviving members of the famous 1948 Invincibles at August 2007, don't have one between them.

Conversely, caps have been collected, bought, borrowed and, indeed, stolen, and for some collectors and contemporary players they have become valuable objects, are insured for many thousands of dollars and kept under lock and key.

By the start of the 21st century the baggy green had become an object of desire compelling owners to re-evaluate their relationship with what was once simply an item of national sporting dress.

'That there are so few of them is what makes them a very special piece,' said Ian Redpath, the celebrated batsman and successful antique dealer at Geelong. 'They don't come out of captivity too often. They are very sought after and those who collect them are very genuine in their desire to have them. It's not like collecting Dinky toys. The baggy green is of national importance.'

For many years the cap could be replaced on request and often was. To some players the blazer had greater significance. To others, it was the short-sleeved jumper or simply the green and gold colours they held so dear.

'I must admit the baggy green was something to be worn just as a blazer was to be worn to go to lunch,' said Neil Harvey, who only rarely wore a cap at the crease or in the field. 'The word memorabilia was not even in the dictionary when I was playing.'

Harvey gave away all his caps bar the 1948 Invincibles baggy green and blazer which, along with the Don Bradman Sykes bat he used in just one match for his unforgettable 112 and 4 not out at Headingley in 1948, is in the proud possession of his daughter Anne.

Among those to receive a baggy green from Harvey were Simpson 'Sammy' Guillen, a member of the exclusive fraternity to have played Test cricket for two countries (West Indies and New Zealand) and St. George rugby league hooker Ernest Harold

'Tiger' Black, who after serious injury served the game as an administrator and renowned broadcaster for commercial radio in Sydney.

Morris gave one to Frank Worrell, the first black captain of the West Indies outside the Caribbean and a statesman among the game's leaders. Another beneficiary was a young Indian boy who made some runs while Morris was in Mumbai for a charity match.

By no means was Black the only prominent member of the media to benefit from the generosity of Australian players. Colin McDonald, who broadcast cricket for the ABC, gave one of his caps to Englishman Brian 'Johnners' Johnston, who was renowned for bringing a touch of vaudeville to his commentary. Following his death in 1994 the family auctioned the cap for charity. Keith Stackpole gave caps to Rex Pullen, a long-serving sports journalist at the then Herald-Sun organisation in Melbourne, and to the family of Mike Williamson, well known in the southern states for his Australian football commentary.

While sympathetic to their predecessors who lost rather than gained money through their association with the game, the modern cricketer finds it difficult to accept the sale of a baggy green.

'I get a little distressed when I see a player selling it off for financial gain,' observed Steve Rixon. 'I just couldn't imagine selling it even in the most difficult times. Other things can be offered but not the cap. Let's keep that sacred.'

'You are never far enough in debt to sell an Australian cap,' said Ross Edwards. 'Never; no matter how much you'd get. Get rid of everything but not the cap. I'm a little ashamed that I swapped mine for a bobby's helmet. It's an iconic emblem. I'd be very surprised, indeed, disappointed, if this wasn't the view of all cricketers. I would have to think less of an Australian cricketer who did not appreciate the reverence of the baggy green. I would be very surprised if this is not a universal feeling.'

Geoff Lawson and Terry Jenner are more pragmatic.

'When I hear of the auctions I don't think that it is crass commercialism I think it is maybe unfortunate that they had to sell them,' said Lawson. 'But if it was a contemporary player earning millions of dollars and selling a cap I would be dirty about that.'

Jenner, who was closely involved in the 50th anniversary of Don Bradman's Invincibles in 1998, said he was encouraged when some of the old players received something worthwhile for their caps. 'I felt sad that they needed to part with them but pleased they got something for them as they got so little out of the game in that way.'

If Edwards felt ashamed about swapping a cap with a member of the English constabulary he was not alone. Doug Walters, Jeff Thomson, Max Walker, Ashley Mallett, David Hookes and Alan Turner also confessed to such a bizarre transaction with a bobby. Such aberrant behaviour was not, however, confined to the early and mid-1970s. At the World Cup in 1979 Rodney Hogg swapped a cap not for a bobby's helmet but for the officer's lapel identification number, baton and handcuffs. 'I should lock myself up, shouldn't I,' conceded Hogg.

Thomson did not stop at a bobby's helmet. In the Caribbean in 1978 he traded a baggy green for the field medals belonging to a monolithic Jamaican policeman and Commonwealth Games athlete who had protected the Australians during the riots at Sabina Park in Kingston during the tour.

'He was a huge bloke who had taken a bullet or two in his time. Can't remember his name,' observed Thomson laconically.

Certainly there is an increasing need for past owners of the baggy green to be philosophical, perhaps even forgiving.

Genial, undemanding Brian Booth encapsulated it best when he observed: 'When you give the baggy green away it is really up to the recipient to do what they want with it.'

Booth has a fond memory of a voice ringing out over the glorious Worcester ground on his first visit to England in 1961.

'When I got my first run I heard someone say: "Congratulations on your first run on English soil." It was (the distinguished English batsman) Tom Graveney and I hold Tom in the highest regard,' said Booth.

Although only directly opposed in three Test matches in 1962-63 they became good friends and Booth happily presented Graveney with a baggy green. In recent years, Booth learnt it had been included in a sale of Graveney's cricket memorabilia.

This is not an uncommon practice. Indeed, in March 2007 at the Nottingham racecourse, the cap Arthur Morris swapped with England leg-spinner Eric Hollies in 1950-51 fetched £3600 at auction.

It is impossible to know how many baggy greens are in existence and their whereabouts. Many are either in the hands or, indeed, have left the hands of the descendants of players, collectors and investors. For instance, it is documented that Australia's 25th Test captain, Ian Johnson, presented his cap to Stuart Surridge after Surrey beat the 1956 Australian team. Surridge died at 74 in 1992. Just months after retiring from Test cricket in 2007 Justin Langer was given Keith Miller's 1956 baggy which had been auctioned in Melbourne in 2006, two years after Miller's death at the age of 84. Allan Border provided a cap for rugby league champion Johnny Raper, while Alan Davidson presented one to tennis ace Neale Fraser who was given to wearing it at the crease for the Melbourne Cricket Club's Club XI.

Before they were required to sign a statutory declaration to replace it many players were given to swapping caps with an opponent although Bob Simpson said it was a practice frowned upon by the game's governors.

Be that as it may, Simpson has the caps of his great pal, the late Ken Barrington (England), Fred Titmus and the late Conrad Hunte (West Indies) from his first stint as Australian captain.

Allan Border, Steve Waugh and Dean Jones managed to build impressive collections without surrendering the baggy greens of greatest importance to them. Border treasures his first cap which he estimates he wore for the first 80 of his then record 156 Test matches, while Jones is particularly enamoured of the cap he donned for his career-defining 210 in the tied Test with India at Chennai in September 1986.

Border has caps worn by Allan Lamb and Wayne Larkins (England), Javed Miandad (Pakistan), Duleep Mendis (Sri Lanka), Paul McEwan (New Zealand), Kepler Wessels (South Africa), Jeff Dujon (West Indies) and Chetan Chauhan (India).

Waugh swapped with Neil Foster (England), Saeed Anwar (Pakistan), Mohammad Azharuddin (India), Hansie Cronje (South Africa) and Ravi Ratnayeke (Sri Lanka). Jones, a garrulous and persuasive soul, swapped jumpers for caps worn by Javed Miandad, Viv Richards (West Indies), Martin Crowe (New Zealand) and Kapil Dev (India). Max Walker has the caps of Derek Underwood (England), Andy Roberts (West Indies) and Dale Hadlee (New Zealand), while Kim Hughes has the caps worn with pride by Mike Brearley (England) and Viv Richards (West Indies), and Graham McKenzie has the cap of England's Welsh fast bowler Jeff Jones.

And so it goes, each cap evoking so many rich memories of summers and deeds long past but never to be forgotten.

MC

3
THE ROAD TO THE BAGGY GREEN

RECENT Australian captains, most notably Mark Taylor and Steve Waugh, have emphasised the significance and uniqueness of wearing the baggy green Australian cricket cap. This famous cap is now an integral part of the Australian cricket team's uniform. However in the years before Federation in 1901 this was not the case.

Before the formation of the Australian Cricket Council (1892-1900), Australian teams playing in England wore a variety of colours because no team uniform existed. The absence of a national cricket organisation in Australia ensured that this situation continued into the early years of Federation.

It wasn't until 1994 that a short paper, 'The Origin of the Green and Gold', published in *Sporting Traditions*, the journal of the Australian Society for Sports History, established that the 1899 Australians in England, captained by Joe Darling, were the first Australian cricket team to adopt these famous colours when they wore a green and gold cap, replete with an Australian coat of arms. They also wore a matching 'gum-tree' green blazer with the coat of arms on the pocket over the heart. The blazer was trimmed with 'wattle' gold.[1]

The distinguished historian Richard Cashman points out that today the baggy green cap is a unique national icon which has achieved almost reverential status. 'It is one of the best-known brands in the country, enjoying a similar pre-eminent status in Australia to the All Black jersey in New Zealand ... The baggy green cap has been treated as an exclusive symbol that includes no sponsor logos and is not available for sale.'[2]

To examine how the cap evolved into its present colour and shape it is necessary to study the various colours and uniform designs worn by the Australian teams that visited Britain in the second half of the 19th century.

The first group of Australian cricketers to tour England was the Aboriginal team of 1868, which was managed by the former Surrey professional Charles Lawrence. This ground-breaking team apparently did not use a standard uniform or team colours. There is no image of the squad in a uniform even though a collage in the Marylebone Cricket Club collection at Lord's shows four of the players wearing a dark, long-sleeved shirt with a light sash or diagonal stripe across the front.[3] This collage also suggests that other players in the team wore a variety of Victorian club colours and caps or just personal cricket attire. However a rare hand-coloured cabinet card produced during the lead-up games in Australia shows each player wearing a distinctly coloured cap. The name of each player associated with each cap is listed at the bottom of the card, allowing ready identification. This was a portent for the future. Today's Australian one-day cricketers, and more recently their opponents, have their names printed on the backs of their shirts. One of the tourists was officially known as 'Red Cap', suggesting that the practice of individually coloured caps for the Aboriginal cricketers was more prevalent than modern historians suppose.

The 1878 Australians wore a uniform of white and sky blue, the colours of the East Melbourne Cricket Club. Their blazers were white with sky blue vertical stripes. The headwear was an unusual white cap with two horizontal sky blue bands without a peak or brim. The cap was shaped like an inverted pudding bowl, a design that might have been borrowed from some English cricket teams, such as I Zingari, or the football teams of Eton and Harrow. An evocative oil painting in the Rex Nan Kivell collection in the National Library of Australia depicting play during the tour's first match, against Willsher's Gentlemen at Chilham Castle in Kent, shows several Australians sporting the round, oddly shaped cap.[4]

Photographs and coloured lithographs of the 1878 tourists demonstrate clearly that there was no logo or coat of arms on their caps or blazers. This is also confirmed by the well-known lithograph by 'Spy' of Fred Spofforth, Australia's opening bowler. This beautiful print clearly shows Spofforth wearing his blue and white cap with matching tie and blazer, standing rather nonchalantly with his hands in his pockets. It was made available with copies of *Vanity Fair* published on 13 August, 1878 and is now a rare collector's item. This seminal tour was a private venture, organised by John Conway, a former Melbourne Cricket Club player. The tour was not sanctioned by the cricket associations of NSW or Victoria. Whether or not the East Melbourne club helped sponsor the tour is unclear as no relevant minutes from the club survive. The use of the club's distinctive colours during the tour does suggest that the club might have contributed in some way.

The Australian tour of 1880 featured blazers with black and magenta vertical stripes. There was no distinctive pocket or coat of arms on the blazer. The very few available photographs of the team show no team cap. Except for the occasional top hat, the players are bare-headed, although they might have worn their club or state caps while fielding. On the way home this team visited North America for a series of matches. A black and white lithograph from an unidentified New York magazine shows individual head and shoulder portraits of the players. Four are wearing caps similar in design to that of the 1878 Australians, except that two thick horizontal circles on the caps appear to be a dark colour which suggests that the caps might have been magenta and black. Importantly the caps display no logo, badge or coat of arms. During this tour the first Test match played on English soil took place at the Oval.

According to Richard Cashman, the famous 1882 Australian team wore the red, black and yellow colours of the 96th Regiment.[5] They enjoyed a resounding victory at the Oval in the only Test played that summer. As Philip Derriman has pointed out, this team might have also worn their Australian club blazers on tour.[6] A lithograph or hand-coloured print reproduced in David Frith's *Pageant of Cricket* depicts some of the players sporting a variety of coloured blazers. Spofforth, Harry Boyle and the captain Billy Murdoch are wearing emerald green blazers with thick dark green vertical stripes.[7] Tom Horan's blazer has dark brown vertical stripes. George Bonnor is the only player not in cricket attire; he is wearing a handsome brown suit. Six of the players are wearing identical dark green skull caps but there is no badge or coat of arms on either the blazers or the caps. This formal group portrait was most likely composed during or soon after the Oval Test, which suggests that the team might have discarded the colours of the 96th Regiment as the tour progressed in favour of the blazers and caps shown in this seemingly official lithograph.

However, if the above picture is a hand-coloured print it must be viewed with some scepticism as it may have been coloured some years after the tour. Whist visiting the Welsh book town of Hay-on-Wye during the 1997 Ashes tour of England this writer noticed the proprietor of a print shop blithely using watercolours on an old black and white newspaper print of the 1886 Australians in England. He was painting their striped blazers in green and gold which, of course, was incorrect. The 1886 team wore magenta, blue and white, the colours of the Melbourne Cricket Club. Old newspaper prints of Australian cricket teams in England can still be found today with incorrect team colours added years later.

The 1884 Australians in England wore caps and blazers of azure blue, identical in tint to the famous colours of the Italian national soccer side, the 'Azzuri'. We have at least three items of evidence to support this assertion. The striking *Vanity Fair* lithograph by Carlo Pelegrini, known as 'Ape', of George Bonnor, the giant Victorian batsman, shows him wearing the azure cap. Tantalisingly the image is a side-on view and shows only a small portion of the badge on Bonnor's cap. The picture shows the part of the badge which is a gold circle enclosing what looks to be the tail of a kangaroo, also in gold, which suggests the presence of an Australian coat of arms on the cap. The other piece of evidence is a beautiful hand-coloured lithograph in a private collection. This Boyle and Scott lithograph, probably composed just after the tour, shows the 1884 Australians in official pose wearing their azure blazers and caps. The Australian coat of arms is also featured but separately in a large circle underneath the image of the players. Close examination of the emblems on the caps and blazers suggests that the design on the cap might be of an emu and a kangaroo holding a shield within a gold circle, as suggested by the Ape photogravure of Bonnor. The blazer pocket was decorated with a coat of arms without the enclosing circle. The shield within the coat of arms contained in clockwise direction the images of a sheep, a sailing ship, a sheaf of wheat and a crossed miner's pick and shovel. These items were divided by a cross containing four of the stars of the Southern Cross. Above the shield was the symbol of the rising sun.

However there is further evidence to suggest that the 1884 Australians may have been the first to wear an Australian coat of arms on their blazers, as a Boyle and Scott lithograph suggests. The Bradman Museum in Bowral has a 'royal blue' blazer with a 'cricketer's coat of arms' on the blazer. The kangaroo is on the right of the shield and the emu on the left with the rising sun above the shield. The order of the emu and kangaroo is the same as in the Boyle and Scott lithograph. The blazer is thought to have belonged to Spofforth and was owned previously by the late CEO of the NSW Cricket Association, Bob Radford, a devotee of cricket history. These three pieces of evidence strongly suggest that the 1884 Australians were the first team to wear a distinctly Australian coat of arms but were not the first to wear 'Advance Australia' on their uniform as this important motto is not on the Spofforth blazer.

The 1886 Australians in England donned the famous magenta, blue and white colours of their sponsor, the Melbourne Cricket Club. The cap and blazer both displayed the well-known MCC emblem.[8] Fortunately for posterity a blazer from this tour is part of the MCC Museum collection. The 1888 Australians were also sponsored by the MCC and wore identical caps and blazers to those worn by their 1886 predecessors.

Before the baggy green ... a postcard of Percy McDonnell's 1888 Ashes party. Before 1899 the colours and style of the cap changed almost every tour. On some occasions, as shown here, various caps were worn.

Photo: courtesy Ronald Cardwell

The 1890 Australians were photographed in England wearing dark blue blazers and caps with gold trim and an Australian coat of arms. This uniform closely resembled that worn by the 1884 side. The motto 'Advance Australia', which was incorporated into this 1890 coat of arms, was very popular throughout the land as the push towards nationhood gathered momentum. Today's cricketers wear baggy green caps with only 'Australia' underneath the coat of arms. The 'Advance Australia' motto was in use on the Victorian goldfields as far back as 1853, the year before the Eureka Stockade uprising. An S.T. Gill painting from that year, depicting the decorations for a subscription ball, housed in the Ballarat Fine Art Gallery, shows the words 'Advance Australia' clearly printed in a scroll with a shield containing the Southern Cross – soon to become the symbol of the Eureka uprising.

The 1893 Australian cricket team, the eighth to tour England, adopted a striking emblem incorporating the four main stars of the Southern Cross within a curved shield. This design is similar to that shown in the S.T. Gill painting 40 years earlier. Each star was joined by a white Crusader-like cross. However there was no use on the shield of either the kangaroo or emu, or the motto 'Advance Australia'. This emblem was sown onto the left blazer pocket and the players' skull caps.[9]

★★★★★

At a meeting of the Australasian Cricket Council in Adelaide on 8 January, 1895, Percy Sheridan (NSW) successfully proposed that the selection of colours for future Australian teams be decided by a subcommittee. Although the council was not a fund-raising body, it was the governing body of cricket in Australia before the Board of Control was formed. Part of the council's charter was 'the regulation of visits of Australian teams to England and elsewhere'. The council also approved the appointment of national selectors. The council's meeting at the Oxford Hotel in Sydney on 8 October, 1895 decided to send an Australian team to England in 1896.

No minutes exist to clarify what recommendations the council's subcommittee on the choice of the Australia XI's colours made nor what influence any decision exerted on the 1896 players. However, the 'Special Correspondent' for *The Sydney Morning Herald* filed this report from Colombo on 1 April, 1896: 'Agreements for the tour were all signed when the Cuzco was about 10 miles out of Albany, and therefore within the jurisdiction of the British Courts, which extend 30 miles from British ports. The team now seems thoroughly satisfied and content that after all the best selection has been made ... The night before Colombo, an important meeting of the team was held in the saloon. The selection committee was voted for, and the result was a little surprising. It consists of Harry Trott (who was elected captain), George Giffen and Syd Gregory. The colours of the team were also decided upon, and are to be the same as those worn by the 1890 team – dark blue coats and caps with gold binding, the Australian arm on each article.'

During the Second Test match at the MCG in January 1898, the Australians wore the dark blue caps of the Victorian XI. At this time, it was customary to wear the colours of the host state team. Mostyn Evan, the South Australian member of the Australasian Cricket Council's subcommittee on the cricket colours, is reported to have suggested 'a very attractive arrangement of green and gold colours' for the forthcoming 1899 tour of England.

The tenth Australian team to tour England obviously took note of Evan's suggestion as they became the first Australian sports team to wear what became our national colours. Shortly after their arrival on the mail-steamer, Ormuz, the Australians raised a green and gold flag at the Inns of Court Hotel in High Holborn, London, their headquarters for the summer.[10] The *Nepean Times* of 10 June, 1899 informed its readers that: 'A great amount of interest was manifested among members of the team when being measured for their blazers (the colours, by the by, are sage green and gold and green with gold braided edge) as to who would have the greatest development. Howell was easily the first with 45 inches. Jones next with 42 inches.'

The decorative menu for the farewell dinner for the 1899 Australians at their London hotel is appropriately tied with deep green and bright gold ribbons, colours which would become synonymous with the emerging spirit of the new nation. From this time, all Australian cricket teams touring England wore dark green blazers and caps with gold trimming, both decorated with the now familiar kangaroo and emu-adorned coat of arms, which was almost identical to that worn by the 1884, 1890 and 1896 Australian sides. This 1899 design featured a sailing ship, a slaughtered sheep, a sheaf of wheat, a miner's pick and shovel within four segments of a shield intersected by stars of the Southern Cross. However, the kangaroo was on the left of the shield and the emu on the right, as it is today. The motto 'Advance Australia' was included underneath in gold wire thread. The green and gold striped blazers worn by the 1993-94 Australian XI were a 'first' but were obviously influenced by Australian club cricketers in the early half of the 20th century. This 1993-94 team, however, wore the traditional baggy green cap, which was almost identical to that worn by Joe Darling's 1899 Australians in England almost a hundred years before.

It was not until after Federation that the green and gold colours of the Australian XI were first seen on home soil. The host team sported our national colours during the Second Test against Archie MacLaren's Englishmen which began at the MCG on 1 January, 1902.[11] These colours were not to be ratified by the infant Board of Control until 1908. Meeting in Melbourne on 29 May, the board passed a motion that the official colours for future Australian cricket teams be 'Gum-tree Green and Gold'. This official sanction for a combination of colours that had been in use for nine years set the seal on the future use of the green and gold on Australian caps and blazers for generations. The cap did not become baggy in appearance until after World War I, players of Victor Trumper's era wearing a tight-fitting green and gold cap.

The 1899 Australian touring side in England began the proud tradition of the green and gold cap and blazer with the cricket style coat of arms (as distinct from the official Australian coat of arms). Confirming cricket's standing as the national game, green and gold would eventually become Australia's official national colours.

Peter Sharpham

* Peter Sharpham was born in Sydney in 1945. A collector of cricket ephemera from the age of 12, he has a master's degree in sports history from Illinois State University and has written two cricket biographies and one tour book.

References

1 *Sporting Traditions*, May 1994 – Peter Sharpham.
2 'Branding of Australian Cricket: Culture, Commerce, Cricket and the baggy green cap', *Sporting Traditions*, November 2006 – Richard Cashman.
3 *The Pictorial History of Australian Cricket* – Jack Pollard, J.M. Dent 1983.
4 Ibid.
5 *The Demon Spofforth* – Richard Cashman, NSWUP, 1990.
6 'The Green and Gold – 100 Years Young', *Wisden Cricketers' Almanack Australia* 1999 – Philip Derriman.
7 *Pageant of Cricket* – David Frith, Macmillan, 1987.
8 *Glorious Innings – Treasures from the Melbourne Cricket Club Collection* – Richard Bouwman, Hutchinson Australia 1987.
9 Pollard, op. cit.
10 Newspaper cutting, NSWCA Library.
11 *History of the Melbourne Cricket Club* – Hugh Field, unpublished manuscript, MCC Library.

4

THE GUM-TREE GREEN AND GOLD

IN a world of instant gratification and increasingly meaningless accolades, the Australian Test cricket cap – colloquially referred to as the baggy green – is a mark of rare distinction, a national icon.

A release in 2006 of limited edition memorabilia by Legends Genuine Memorabilia[1] was entitled 'The Pride of the Baggy Green'. This lithograph[2] was the genesis of the research that evolved into this book. During this project it became clear that there had been little research into the cap's evolution and history.

The timeline of caps in the lithograph (reproduced on this book's back cover) started with Victor Trumper and continued through to Don Bradman – the game's greatest player – and the cap he wore when he first captained Australia. The trilogy was completed with the cap of the baggy green's most public face, Steve Waugh. These caps are truly the highlight of this unique, unifying symbol. They tell the fascinating story of the cap's evolution and represent both the history of the baggy green and of Australian Test cricket.

The current cap can be traced back to the cap and colours adopted by the visionary members of the 1899 touring team to England. In one of cricket's serendipitous coincidences, the green cap with the Australian cricket coat of arms made its Test debut in the first Test at Trent Bridge, Nottingham

– as did Victor Trumper, the game's most stylish batsman and a great admirer of the Australian cap. His contemporary, Clem Hill, wrote that Trumper formed a strong attachment to his cap: 'It was bottle green, but nevertheless he stuck to it to the end and there was always no end of bother if (Reg) Duff or some of the other humorists of the side got hold of the cap and hid it.'[3]

The colours adopted by the members of this team before the Tests – the green and gold – became the colours for all Australian sporting teams. While the game's administrators did not officially adopt the 'gum-tree green and gold' colours and coat of arms until 1908, these 1899 colours and design are different from and predated the current Australian Commonwealth coat of arms, which was adopted in 1912. The cricket coat of arms is one of the few pre-Federation symbols in use today.

Baggies on the march … the powerful Australian team in England in 1921. The great all-rounder Jack Gregory, second from left back row, seems to be wearing his old skull cap while his teammates have adopted the newer baggy style cap which is still worn today. **Photo: courtesy Ronald Cardwell**

The official Australian livery was blue and gold until 1984, when the Hawke government adopted green and gold as the national colours. The decision of the 1899 team to incorporate these colours with the coat of arms was a defining moment in Australian sport as the colours were adopted by the Australian Olympic team in 1908, the Australian rugby league Kangaroos in 1928, and rugby union's Wallabies the year after.

The long ancestry of the baggy green and the continuity in its design mean that there is a strong sense of legacy and obligation for those selected as an Australian Test cricketer. Allan Border, a driving force behind the first reunion of Australian Test cricketers, held in Sydney in 2000, revealed his inspiration: 'In Australian cricket, one of our strengths has always been a good team spirit. Don Bradman played in a baggy green, so did Victor Trumper and all the blokes over the years. So there's a realisation when you get given that cap you're part of something special.'[4]

The baggy green has a uniquely Australian feel. Originally, it was a skull cap, like those commonly worn in England. From 1920 however the cap had a baggy or Australian style. Generally this term is applied to all Test caps from 1899. The distribution of the Test and state caps reflects the egalitarian nature of Australian society. Every player receives a cap on selection, whereas in England caps are awarded to denote status and seniority. A player could remain 'uncapped' even after years of representing his county.[5]

This sense that Australian values, history and legacy are represented in the cap has re-emerged in the past decade. In November 1994, Mark Taylor instituted the practice of the whole team wearing the cap during the first fielding session of each Test match.[6] Recently Steve Waugh said that he had suggested this initiative in a team meeting. In any case, Waugh heightened the public perception of the players' respect for the cap when he wore his baggy green until it almost fell apart. He ignored calls to replace the cap although he did bow to pressure and had the peak repaired by Albion in 2002. Waugh received more than one baggy green cap during his career and certainly wore more than one over this 20-year period, though it is certainly true he wore the one cap for the vast majority of his career. This was the cap which was repaired.

Now each new Test player is handed his baggy green by a former player in a ceremony on the morning of his first Test. 'It is such a special time for a player and the old procedure certainly lacked polish,'[7] Taylor said. The formal ceremony instituted by Taylor in 1996 was refined by Waugh, who thought a former Australian Test player should do the presentation. This practice has been copied by the Wallabies and South Africa's Springboks.

In an age when professional sports are inextricably linked to sponsorship, the baggy green and the team blazer stand alone in their purity. Cricket Australia has steadfastly refused to commercialise the cap by putting sponsors' logos on it. And it has never offered replicas for sale, thereby ensuring that no imitation can sully this most prestigious of prizes.

Steve Waugh reinforced this when discussing his cap's repair: 'It gives me power and the team aura. It's something people recognise and respect and, most importantly, it has never been commercialised in any way, nor does it have sponsor logos on it.'[8]

A small replica cap was specially produced for former players and presented to them at a reunion in 2003. These caps were to uniquely bear the players' Test numbers, which were to be embroidered on the back but logistical complexities prevented that. A plaque on each presentation, however, listed each player's Test number. Bill Brown, a former Test captain, member of the 1948 Invincibles, and at the time Australia's oldest Test player, expressed his pleasure in receiving a new cap, as he had not kept any old ones. 'I don't know what happened. I probably gave them away. We valued the caps

Still the leading icon ... Ricky Ponting, Australia's 42nd captain, in today's cap.
Photo: Getty Images

when we received them, but they seem to have become more special in recent times.'[9]

Receiving a baggy green is recognition of your acceptance into the highest level of Australian cricket – a cause for much celebration and congratulations. Yet it is also a time for reflection, for the cap is a reminder of all those who have gone before. The victories and losses, euphoria and heartache are all interlaced in the very fibres of that flannel halo, ensuring that all who wear it are entrusted with a legacy and responsibility of lasting national importance.

To many, Steve Waugh personifies the cap and the importance of its legacy. 'The ultimate goal is to wear the baggy green cap. There's something special about putting that cap on – for me anyway. There's no way you will catch me wearing a white hat. The cap's always on my head. There's an aura about the Australian cap.'[10]

As with any symbol, the baggy green's meaning is personal. For some it carries similar themes but with different emphasis to Waugh's. To Ian Chappell, the message behind the symbolism of the cap is most important. In his foreword to Viv Jenkins's photographic collection, *The Baggy Green*, written in 1998, Chappell states: 'The baggy green, Australian's cricket cap, is more a testimony to the characters who have worn it than a symbol of prestige. If it was more of the latter, then one former player wouldn't have worn his cap to protect his head while painting and four ex-Australian captains that I know of would have retained at least one of their hard-earned items of headwear. Nevertheless, in recent times the baggy green has gained in status. This has occurred because of the price paid for Victor Trumper's cap, the much-publicised search for one of Sir Donald Bradman's Test caps, and the tradition that has developed in the last couple of years where a new player is presented with his cap by the captain on the first morning of the Test. However, I'm sure that even the players who have grown up under this tradition will still remember the characters they played with long after they've forgotten where they stored their baggy green.'

The players of previous eras certainly respected the cap and the 'club' that it signified but, as Chappell acknowledged, the emphasis changed dramatically in the few years up to 1998.

*****

The baggy green of the new millennium is instantly recognisable as that worn throughout most of the 20th century. There have been some changes over the years but generally these have been short-lived; a few have been more enduring. The 1899 cap and the modern cap bear some differences – hence the introduction of the century-old replica in 2000 as an intentional and dramatic point of difference.

The current cap is hand-crafted exclusively under licence by Albion Hat and Cap Company Pty Ltd. It is 100 per cent Australian wool and is officially described as 'bottle green woollen flannel'. Early manufacturers were Potts and Wilkinson in 1899, George Lewin & Co of London Bridge in 1912, Rowan Glasgow in 1921, Harding's Mercery in 1924-25 and 1928-29, and Scholium who made the 1930 touring cap. Some touring caps were made in Britain until a long-term supplier was found. The Farmer's Sydney label appeared on the cap from 1931-32 until the early 1970s, when the label reflected that the licence and production had been entrusted to Albion. Albion had produced the cap for Farmer's since the 1950s.

The minutes of cricket's administrative body since 1899 contain scant mentions of the cap's manufacturer.[11] At the board meeting of December 30 and 31, 1931, and January 1, 1932, it was recorded that 'a tender for production of caps and blazers was accepted from Farmer's. Farmer's had offered to do the job for 5 pounds 10 shillings and sixpence, beating other tenderers David Jones and Hardings.'

Another mention from the board meeting of September 1946 notes that 'the cost of Farmer's services was disaggregated as follows: blazers 2 pounds 19 shillings and sixpence, pocket badge 1 pound 5 shillings, caps 11 shillings and sixpence'.

These notes were purely administrative confirmations, with no hint that the cap was anything more than just another piece of apparel, such as sweaters or boots.

Albion continues to use the original patterns and wooden blocks to cut the panels for their five standard sizes, and there is provision for players to have a cap custom-made to ensure a perfect fit. In the past 10 years, there has been a continuing dialogue between Albion and the players. Caps are now adjusted once they have been worn for some time, and more recently, Albion began steam-cleaning and repairing any caps worn for 100 or more Tests. This process ensures that the caps remain comfortable and presentable.

The cap's essential elements are its shape, its cloth, the components of the coat of arms – the shield, scroll and crest – and any use of dates. All of these have changed at times

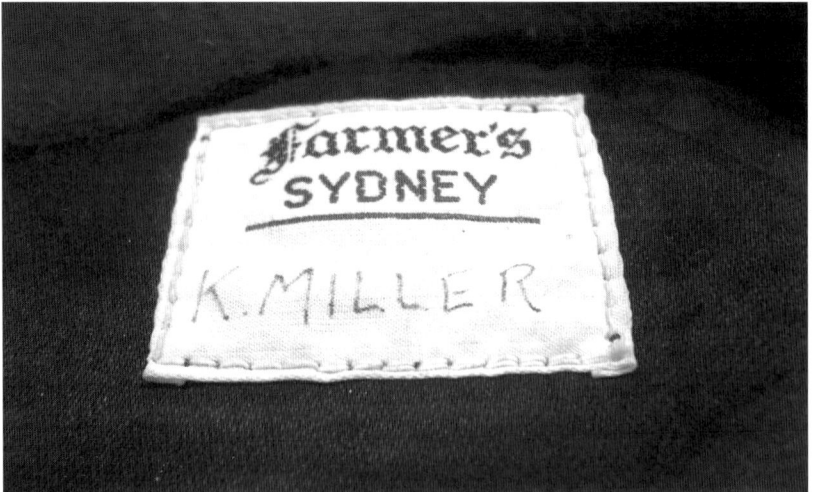

Tagged … the label of Farmer's department store appeared inside the cap for 40 years from 1931-32. The charismatic all-rounder Keith Miller played 55 Test matches between 1946 and 1956. **Photo: courtesy Legends**

over the years and the baggy green, although presented as a constant, has in fact been a work in progress.

With the cricket board's minutes silent as to the changes over the years, we can assume that these occurred for a variety of pragmatic reasons, often made by administrators or the manufacturers. Before computerised embroidery machines, the sewing was done by hand, therefore design variations – for example, in the shape and size of the kangaroo and emu on the coat of arms – occurred depending on the person embroidering them. Changes in the company manufacturing the cap in the 1920s and 1930s also produced variations.

From 1899 the shape of the cap evolved from 'skull' to 'baggy' and the material from velvet to woollen flannel. Why and when did the Test cap become 'baggy'? It would appear that no conscious decision was made; subtle shifts occurred based on prevailing fashion.

The design of headwear varied greatly in the latter part of the 19th century. There were top hats, pill boxes, pudding tops and skull caps. This variety was reflected on the cricket field. The first Test caps in 1878 contained no peak and tight skull caps were in vogue from 1890 until the 1909 Ashes tour. The 1912 cap appears to be somewhat fuller but not yet fully baggy. With the cessation of tours during World War I, Australia's next Test series was not until 1920. In this home series, most of the Australians wore a baggy style cap and, strictly, this was when the baggy green was born.

Supporting the theory that fashion had a role in the cap's evolution, the photographs taken by Frank Laver, the player-manager of the 1905 tourists[12] show the playing cap as being very tight. But interspersed with these photos are images of the same players in daywear sporting fuller styled caps. Clearly this style was favoured by the players away from the field.

Given the intensity of the Australian sun compared to England's, a larger cap with a peak that provided some shade for the face would have been favoured by cricketers. The adoption of a home-grown design also reflected a growing confidence in being distinctly Australian and not slavishly adopting the trends of the mother country. The baggy style was quickly identified with Australians, in stark contrast to the multitude of caps worn by Englishmen.

An article on the great Australian batsman Charlie Macartney by D. J. Knight, published in *Country Life* on 17 June, 1926, states: '... lastly, surmounting all – the cap. There are many cricketers that one cannot truly picture in the mind's eye without the headgear which seems inseparable from, and without which they would no longer seem to retain their personality. Plum Warner at Lord's without his harlequin cap (like Jacob's coat of many colours) is unthinkable – it is no longer 'Plum', but some stranger, unrecognisable, unfamiliar, almost unfriendly. Macartney is no exception – the little eager bird-like figure, not unlike a perky cock sparrow, is completed and adorned with the queer (sic) cap of his country, which seems always too large for him, and whose peak, shaped like a jockey's, seems to dominate and envelope the whole of his figure.'[13]

The baggy shape is achieved in the final stages of manufacture. Beginning its life as eight panels and a peak, the cap is sewn together, sized, blocked and finally tacked. This involves pulling the cap over the peak and sewing it down with four tacks (stitches). This gives it the unique baggy appearance. During the 1997 Ashes series, there were suggestions that the cap's shape was changing.[14] Albion and the Australian team manager, Alan Crompton, confirmed that the caps were being made the same way with the same block and patterns. Two years later[15] Glenn McGrath was identified as the culprit who had lifted the crown and inadvertently detached the stitches. This highlighted the vigilant nature of those watching to ensure that the cap remains the same. The issue that evokes passion is the fact that the cap has not changed since the 1930s and that it is a 'symbolic torch that one generation of Australian players passes on to the next. It is its unchangeability that sets it apart.'[16]

Judging by the caps still in existence, the 1899 version was the only one produced in velvet. Subsequent caps, namely the 1907 and 1909 ones, were made of a woven cotton material. Discussion with Albion, the manufacturer of the 2000 skull cap, revealed that embroidering onto velvet is a difficult operation.[17] It is possible that these difficulties precluded velvet's continued use. Cost may also have been a factor. The 1930 Scholium-manufactured cap had two metal punch holes on either side, presumably for ventilation. This is the only cap with this feature.

Even in the 21st century (the cap's third century) the players continue to help mould its appearance. Traditionally, Albion lined the cap with its generic inner label. This is a circular cloth patch, bearing the words: 'Albion, C&D, official suppliers to South African Cricket Union, New Zealand Cricket, Australian Cricket Board'. Albion learned that Justin Langer had blotted out the references on his cap's label to South Africa and New Zealand. In 2002 Albion redesigned the label and the baggy green now proudly states 'Official Australian Test cap'. Albion then took the specialisation a step further and designed the label in such a way that the players' Test numbers could be heat-sealed onto the interior.[18] This change was not embraced as tour managers need to take several spare caps of varying sizes to ensure there is a good fit for any debutant. Again, pragmatism affected the cap's appearance.

★★★★★

The components of the baggy's coat of arms have also evolved. The scroll, set below the shield and originally blue, featured the words 'Advance Australia'. The colour changed to red soon after, and then in the early 1930s 'Advance' was dropped. The historian Richard Cashman suggests that this was done following a directive from the Commonwealth government.[19] This seems possible as the original 1908 Australian coat of arms did contain 'Advance Australia' but the 1912 (the current version) used 'Australia' only.

Similar coats of arms were used by sports, towns and cities from the 1850s and reflected important elements of Australian life and history: commerce, immigration, the production of sheep and wheat, and the minerals extracted from the ground – represented by picks. These elements of the shield are set around a Southern Cross and were supported by the uniquely Australian animals, a kangaroo and an emu, set below the crest – a rising sun indicating a new dawn – and above the inspiring 'Advance Australia', reflecting the aspirations of the emerging nation.

The order of the four symbols was altered soon after 1899. On that cap the colours behind the symbols were blue, white, red and white clockwise from top left (as on the current cap) but the order of the symbols embroidered were firstly a ship, a sheep, wheat and a pick. Since 1909 at least, the sheep and ship symbols have been reversed. Initially the cross containing the white 'Southern Cross' stars was gold, but since 1909 has been embroidered in blue.

It appears that the cap carried a different coat of arms from the 1910-11 home Test series against South Africa to the 1912 triangular series in England. Photographs of these teams and a 1912 cap Edgar Mayne cap held by the National Museum of Australia show that the shield was white with a red cross enclosed. A kangaroo and an emu supported the shield with a star on top. This design was the first official coat of arms for the newly federated Australia. This was granted by Edward VII in a royal warrant on 7 May, 1908. Below the shield was 'Advance Australia'. It is possible that it was adopted so the cap would match the official coat of arms. There is no mention of this in the board minutes, but one theory about the change is that the newly formed Board of Control was exerting its authority over

A variation ... fast bowler Albert 'Tibby' Cotter, who was killed by a sniper at Beersheba in Palestine in the Great War, strikes a genial pose at the Lord's Nursery in 1909. Note that the kangaroo is to the right of the coat of arms on this cap.
Photo: courtesy Ronald Cardwell

the players. From 1905 to 1912 there were continual disputes between the Test players and the new board. One example of the friction concerned the 1909 tour to Britain. As Gideon Haigh noted: 'Even the team's notepaper caused irritation: (team manager William) McElhone insisted it bear the board's letterhead alongside the Australian XI symbol, which Laver griped would "spoil the looks of the neat and pretty heading".'[20]

Clearly the players, who previously toured as entrepreneurs sharing tour profits, resented the board's attempt to take control. But this dispute also shows that the players felt the Australia XI symbol – the coat of arms on the cap – was their symbol, not the board's. The fact that the players had created the emblem would have reinforced this sense of ownership. The cap may well have been a symbolic battlefield between two sides keen to establish their legitimacy. At the time people often asked whether the players were representing the board or the nation. This series of disputes culminated in Victor Trumper, Warwick Armstrong, Vernon Ransford, Albert Cotter, Clem Hill and Hanson Carter – called 'the big six' because of their high standing in Australian cricket – refusing to accept the board's conditions for touring Britain in 1912.

The official Australian coat of arms of 1908 made no reference to the states and several alterations were suggested. These suggestions resulted in the current Commonwealth coat of arms which was proclaimed, again by royal warrant, by George V on 19 September, 1912. Significantly this has just 'Australia' in the wreath. We have no explanation why the 1908 coat of arms was used by the cricket board for the cap after 1910, and why the board reverted to the original 1899 cricket version after World War I. It remains a mystery why the official coat of arms of 1912 was not adopted by cricket, as it was by other sports.

The shape of the shield has also varied. Generally, it has been presented as it is today – wider at the top and bottom with a narrow waist. In 1928-29 and again in 1930 the shield was even wider at the top and tapered to a point at the bottom. Similarly, the shape and size of the rising sun, kangaroo and emu have changed. The basic design of the shield supported by the kangaroo and emu was used from 1884, possibly earlier. The 1893 Australian team sported a shield on the cap and blazer, and the 1896 side included a kangaroo and emu. The original and current coat of arms has the kangaroo on the left and the emu on the right but this positioning was reversed for the 1905, 1907-08 and 1909 teams.

Originally, the coat of arms was made with what is known as bullion embroidery, coloured metallic wire and silk thread. This is shown in intricate detail on the Trumper and Bradman caps as it was used up to 1938, the last tour before World War II. From 1946-47 to the current day, the embroidery has been comprised solely of cotton thread, although auction houses erroneously describe this as silk thread.

There was one season when the Australian cap carried a different coat of arms. The 1963-64 cap sported the official Australian coat of arms, as set out in the 1912 royal warrant. This cap, for the series against South Africa, carried the kangaroo, emu and 'Australia' ribbon, and sported the Commonwealth shield, which contains the individual crests of the six states – not the ship, sheep etc. The rising sun was replaced with a six-pointed star (the Commonwealth star has seven points). This crest, which sat on top of a blue and gold wreath, was featured on the blazer as well, and appears to have been used only for that season.

There is no official explanation for this although one theory is that the coat of arms was replaced in response to the controversy over that summer's tour by the South Africans. South Africa had just been expelled from the ICC due to its apartheid policy and there was some dispute about the Test status of the series. A decision may have been taken to change the emblems to signify that the XI were representing Australia and not the Australian Board of Control.

From 1930 to 1972, the date of each series was embroidered on the cap in the traditional place – below the scroll. There have been some exceptions to this: in 1909 the date was woven into the ribbon in the middle of 'Advance' and 'Australia'; in 1931-32, as modelled in a classic photo of Bradman, the date appeared on either side of the newly singular 'Australia'. We have no cap or image from 1930-31 but as the Farmer's tender was accepted during the New Year's Test in 1931-32, it seems that this was the first year of Farmer's manufacture and the board was merely ratifying what the administration had enacted. This may explain the new design with the dates either side of 'Australia'. What is known is that from 1932-33 to 1972 the cap's design remained the same (barring the 1963-64 cap). The current cap retains this design, with the lack of date and cotton thread the only changes from Bodyline days.

Traditionally players received numerous caps, especially when they were dated. A new cap was awarded for each series, and on some tours, notably the 1948 tour, players received two caps. This fact has only recently been uncovered. The accepted wisdom had been that one cap was issued for each series. The State Library of South Australia inquired into the issuing of caps when they were offered a 'second' Bradman 1948 cap in 2004.

The library's Bradman website states: 'The library approached Bradman's 1948 Invincibles teammates, Sam Loxton and Ron Hammence. Both clearly recalled receiving two caps for the tour in question. Also contacted was Barry Jarman, who kept wicket for Australia in the 1960s. He similarly recalled receiving two caps for each of the 1961, 1964 and 1968 tours of England.'

The issuing of two caps on the 1948 tour became irrefutable when, in July 2004, the former CEO of the South Australian Cricket Association, the late Barry Gibbs, uncovered the existence of an original players' contract for that tour. He obtained a copy and found that paragraph 32 stated: 'The Board shall provide each player with a blazer, two caps, sweater and tie.' [21]

In the 1970s and 1980s the awarding of caps was not done automatically each season, although players from that era received several caps during their career. Albion's former managing director Tony Henson said that repeated requests for replacement caps by two senior players in the early 1980s alerted him to the possibility that the demand by the public for caps was becoming excessive. At his request the board set down rules for the allocation of baggy greens.[22]

Since the 1990s the current policy, which is strictly enforced, stipulates that a player is presented with a cap on debut and that this will be his only cap unless it is stolen or lost, or if it needs to be replaced due to excessive wear.

In July 2007 Cricket Australia's kit manager, Adam Fraser, provided a copy of this policy: 'The baggy green is obviously presented to each player on the ground before the commencement of the first Test they're selected to play in. CA policy is that the baggy green shall not be replaced unless stolen or severely damaged. Players are required to fill in a form that verifies that their baggy has been lost, stolen or damaged before consideration is given to issuing a new one. Generally, we find that players are very protective of their baggy greens and don't like to have them replaced.'

Now the awarding of a cap has evolved into a ceremony whereby a past player makes the presentation to the debutant, again reinforcing the legacy of the elite club of Australia Test cricketers. At the time of writing this elite club has only 399 members. Western Australia's Chris Rogers was Australian Test player No. 399.

In a further mark of respect for the cap, Albion C&D make and present to each player a bag to house the cap, further protecting it. Embroidered upon the bag is the player's name and Test number.

*****

Three variations of the baggy green – ceremonial but match versions – have been made.

In the 1988 Bicentennial Test against England in Sydney, the Australians wore a white baggy cap with green piping. This cap had a unique Bicentennial-inspired logo with the lion and kangaroo facing each other over a wicket. The English players were also presented with a baggy white as a souvenir.

The resurgence of interest in the cap and its history resulted in replica commemorative caps being designed for the Sydney New Year's Day Tests of 2000 and 2001. These caps paid homage to previous designs – the first was a replica of the 1900 velvet skull cap.[23]

'This is the first Test of the new millennium and we thought we'd do something to celebrate playing for Australia,' Steve Waugh said. 'A couple of weeks ago I thought: "The first Test of the new millennium, what can we do to celebrate the fact we are playing for Australia?" It's a skull cap and it's a little bit different to the cap we wear now. It seems to give the players more character straightaway. You have got to know where you have come from to know where you are going. I think that's important in sport.'[24]

The 2000 velvet cap made by Albion used a lurex thread which gave it a slightly metallic sheen. It was a direct copy of the 1899 Trumper cap auctioned by Christies Australia in 1997.

The 2001 commemorative cap celebrated the Centenary of Australia's Federation on 1 January, 1901. This was a baggy green with yellow piping. While this design was depicted on cigarette cards of the Australian team issued in 1905,[25] it appears to be poetic licence as records suggest this style was never worn by an Australian Test team. The embroidery below the coat of arms on the 2001 commemorative says: 'Centenary of Federation Test Match 2001'.

The most recent variation was made for the inaugural ICC Super Series when the Australians, as the world's highest ranked team, played the World XI in a ODI series and a Test match in October 2005. The cap, while the normal design, had the details for this series embroidered on its back panel, 'ICC Super Series Australia v World XI'.

State associations and museums received presentation copies of the 2000 and 2001 caps. This was a generous and far-sighted initiative by the ACB as the Western Australian Cricket Association, for instance, had no caps in its collection. The two donated formed the basis of a collection which recently acquired the baggy green belonging to West Australian Keith Slater, who played one Test against England in 1958-59.

Two other Test caps have recently been produced, but only as prototypes that were not approved by Cricket Australia. The first was submitted by Albion to CA to commemorate the first Test between Australia and Bangladesh, which was played in Darwin in July 2003. It was made from the candy stripe material used in the blazers in the late 1990s. The second was made for the ICC Test match played in Sydney in October 2005. It was a green cap with Petersham ribbon in concentric circles around the cap. There may well be a halt to dramatically different caps for a while.

*****

Behind the scenes the ACB and more recently Cricket Australia have grappled with the problem of protecting its trade marks, images and intellectual property from unauthorised use. In the late 1990s Coopers Brewing Company produced a marketing poster in which baggy green caps were portrayed as bottle tops on pictures of bottled beer.[26] Entitled 'Cooper's salutes some of Australia's most famous green caps', it listed all the post-war Test captains' names under a cap. The board had not approved this use of its intellectual property and received no royalty from this promotion. More importantly the use of the caps to promote a product cut across existing sponsorship deals and was a significant threat to a legitimate sponsor's rights. Legal advice given to the board indicated that it had little recourse because trade mark protection was not available as coats of arms were 'prohibited marks'. Cricket Australia then registered a distinct brand which it could use for all its uniforms, memorabilia and merchandise. Eventually legal protection was granted to Cricket Australia for its coat of arms and the term 'baggy green'.

In 2002-03 the Australian Cricket Board re-branded itself as Cricket Australia and a new logo was created. The board's annual report said: 'The new brand mark incorporates the kangaroo and emu from the traditional cricket coat of arms, the Southern Cross, Australia's green and gold colours and a sunburst, representing the traditional relationship between cricket and the Australian summer.'

Importantly ... 'the cherished baggy green cap has not changed. After consultation with players and other stakeholders about a suitable approach for Australia's most famous cap, it was agreed that the iconic baggy green should remain in its current form. It will keep the traditional cricket coat of arms emblem.'[27]

The traditional coat of arms was also retained on the helmet. The new CA logo is now used on the Test and ODI shirts, Test jumpers and the ODI cap. Tradition had partially defeated a considerable commercial problem. Supported by the players, the cap, in conjunction with the coat of arms, proved too powerful a symbol to be discarded. However the coat of arms was removed from the shirts, sunhat and jumper due to market pressures.

While the legal question regarding the protection of trade marks and brands was resolved there were still commercial reasons to reinvent the logo. Part of the reasoning was that the cricket associations of the states would adopt the design and base their logos on it. Thus the new CA tagline 'The Backyard to the Baggy Green' could then be seen on all cricket branding. A quick look however at each state association's websites shows that the Northern Territory is the only one to adopt CA's template. Despite the merits of the plan the other associations chose to retain the benefits that had already accrued from their own logos.

★★★★★

Australia's rigid non-commercialisation of the Test cap is at odds with the traditions of other countries.

In England players such as Plum Warner, Douglas Jardine and A.P.F. Chapman played Test cricket in a club or college cap. In 1971 A.J.M. Hewitt wrote: 'Always there was a remarkable display of coloured caps at country house cricket and the identity of the amateurs, who appeared intermittently in first-class cricket, could as a rule be deduced from the caps or sweaters they sported. These caps might, on occasions, become dramatically symbolic as, for instance, the harlequin cap of D.R. Jardine that so provoked the Sydney "Hillites".'[28]

As recently as 1996 the English county Surrey still had a system where the awarding of a cap created a professional elite. The former Australian fast bowler and current Cricket NSW chief executive, David Gilbert, found that when he arrived at the Oval in 1996 capped and uncapped players changed on either side of 'the Surrey wall', a partition that dominated the dressing room.[29] Gilbert had the wall removed. The England team in the 1990s would take the field in a variety of caps – some faded, some baseball style. This was understandable given the amateur/professional dichotomy of English cricket and the resulting dress conventions, and also the fact that the England touring cap was different from the one worn at home. Tours used to be undertaken as the Marylebone Cricket Club (MCC) until the 1960s and the touring cap was blue with a St George and dragon emblem; the home cap sported three lions under a crown.

Indian cricket could also learn from the Australian attitude to its cap and traditions. In 2000 Sunil Gavaskar bemoaned the variety of caps worn and the haphazard respect for the Indian cap and logo. 'There are many lessons the Indian team can learn from this tour. One of them is the respect for tradition ... The Indians should take a leaf out of their opponent's book on matters like Australia's adoption of the 1900-style cap for the final Test.'[30]

Gavaskar was upset that a specially designed player-only cap was given to members of the media covering the tour. He believed a 3-0 defeat by Australia came as no surprise when pride in playing for your country was so diminished. The Indians wore three types of caps: the standard type, others with the players' names embroidered on them, and vice-captain Sourav Ganguly's cap carried advertising as well as his name.

An interesting article by Rohit Brijnath appeared in *Sportstar* magazine in 2001. Comparing Australia and India and the traditions of the two cricket teams he wrote: 'Paradoxically, Australia, a land of unending sameness, culturally not so much impoverished as similar, worships tradition and finds great strength in ritual when it comes to sport.'

Brijnath then set out the various Australian cricket rituals: the cap presentation, the singing by the players of *Under the Southern Cross* after every Test win, bowlers holding the ball up after five-wicket hauls and the Test numbers on the shirts. He quoted Gavaskar from the story above and suggested: 'Not everything demands imitation ... but to dismiss Australia's rituals as foreign, thus useless (as we tend to) is an act of ignorance. Any ritual that binds a team together into a purposeful, proud unit is worth embracing. Any custom that links India's cricketing generations is worth starting.'[31]

As a point of difference, Nasser Hussain noted in his autobiography, *Playing with Fire*: 'Waugh could overdo the love of the baggy green cap. He wore it to Wimbledon (in 1997) to support Australian tennis players and I felt it was a bit of a "look at me" sort of thing. I hated it when an Australian would tell you they cared more or had a mental edge over us. No one cared more about playing for his country than me or most of the men I played with for England. Australia had the edge because they were better, much better at times; that was the bottom line.'

While these are understandable sentiments it should be noted that the recognition of the baggy green's traditions, including its wearing and presentation, were devised to produce a better team. The Australians might have had more talent but undoubtedly the cap and its 'new traditions' contributed to this performance.

The final word comes from Steve Waugh, the man who personified the Australian cap in this period and intertwined past traditions with the demands of the present. 'The ultimate goal is to wear the baggy green cap. There's something special about putting that cap on – for me anyway. There's no way you will catch me wearing a white hat. The cap's always on my head. There's an aura about the Australian cap.' [32]

MF

References

1 Michael Fahey, the co-author, is a shareholder of and consultant to Legends.
2 A limited edition of 500, 'The Pride of the Baggy Green', was signed by Steve Waugh and contained an actual swatch of baggy green material with the coat of arms, supplied by the cap's maker, Albion Hat & Cap Company.
3 *Wisden Cricketers' Almanack Australia*, 1999, 'The Green and Gold – 100 Years Young' – Philip Derriman. This is quoted from a letter dated 25/5/1910.
4 *The Australian*, 23/12/1999. 'Australia's greats to dine out on good memories' – Malcolm Conn.
5 *Wisden Cricket Monthly*, June 2000. 'Classless at New Road' – Emma John.
6 *Wisden Cricketers' Almanack Australia*, 1999. 'The Green and Gold – 100 Years Young' – Philip Derriman.
7 *The Australian*, 12/7/2003. 'So proud to be capped and numbered' – Mike Coward.
8 *The Daily Telegraph*, 21/11/2002, 'If the cap's fixed and still fits I'll wear it' – Steve Waugh.
9 SMH, 11/7/2003. 'A baggy green for Invincible Bill, and that youngster Brett' – Tony Stephens
10 SMH, 12/7/2003. 'Wearing of the green bags a place in our soul' – Tony Stephens.
11 Minutes and citations were supplied by Gideon Haigh for the official history of Cricket Australia.
12 Melbourne Cricket Club Museum, Frank Laver Collection.

13 *Charlie Macartney: Cricket's 'Governor-General'* – Peter Sharpham, Walla Walla Press 2004.
14 SMH, 10/7/97. 'The cap fits, so wear it properly' – Philip Derriman.
15 *Wisden Cricketers' Almanack Australia*, 1999, 'The Green and Gold – 10 years young' – Philip Derriman.
16 Ibid.
17 Discussion with Ross Barrat of Albion.
18 SMH, Nov 2002, "Baggy green gets a personalised touch" – David Sygall.
19 *Sport in the National Imagination*, Walla Walla Press 2002 – Richard Cashman.
20 *The Big Ship: Warwick Armstrong and the Making of Modern Cricket* – Gideon Haigh, Text Publishing 2001.
21 www.slsa.gov.au/bradman/cap
22 *The Baggy Green* – Viv Jenkins, New Holland 1998.
23 Only 24 caps were made, one for each player, one for each state association and the ACB and several for museums. *Inside Edge*, Feb 2000 – Malcolm Conn.
24 *The Daily Telegraph*, 2/1/2000 – 'If the old Aussie cap fits, wear it'.
25 Australian cricket team 1905 – 15 unnumbered cards issued by Snider and Abrahams 1905.
26 A poster signed by 16 of the 19 captains listed was valued by Michael Fahey in 'What's it worth?' a column in the Legends publication *The Sporting Collector*, edition No. 4, 2002.
27 'Re-branding Australian Cricket' – Cricket Australia, 2002-03 annual report.
28 *Playfair Cricket Monthly*, Feb 1971, 'Cricket caps, once a symbol, are not in the fashion these days' – A. J. M. Hewitt.
29 *Wisden Cricket Monthly*, June 2000, 'Classless at New Road' – Emma John.
30 *Inside Edge*, Feb 2000, 'Green with envy' – Malcolm Conn.
31 *Sportstar*, 10-16/11/2001, 'The Importance of Rituals' – Rohit Brijnath.
32 SMH, 12/7/2003, 'Wearing of the green bags a place in our soul' – Tony Stephens.

— SHOW AND TELL —

Not all baggy greens repose behind thick glass in museums, bank vaults and safety deposit boxes, or are secreted in the homes of players and collectors.

Indeed, there are a handful of owners who insist on sharing their cap with disparate groups within the community – from wide-eyed schoolchildren in classrooms to wide-eyed adults in corporate boardrooms.

It is what the folksy raconteur, motivator, author and former ungainly paceman Max Walker calls 'dream time' or 'theatre of the mind'.

And much like Australia's 37th Test captain, Kim Hughes, who focuses on the cap in special presentations to schoolchildren and businessmen alike, Walker has a rich collection of stories about the profound impact of the cap on Australians young and old.

Some want to touch the baggy green and run their fingers across it. For them touching is believing. More want to be photographed wearing it and angled in the style of their favourite player. Others simply want to see it at close range but feel strongly they should not touch it just as they would not touch a religious icon. They are overawed in its presence.

Walker, a charismatic bear of a man who played 34 Tests between 1972 and 1977, on special occasions produces his baggy green from a brown paper bag to graphically illustrate a story from his youth or his quest to reach the elite level of the game.

'I used to dream in technicolour,' said Walker. 'And it was a cinemascope dream of owning a baggy green. I could feel the texture of the cap in my dreams; run my fingers over the coat of arms and the gold braid.

'When I got the green baggy (for his first Test against Pakistan at Melbourne in December 1972) I just couldn't wait to tell someone. I got home to Camberwell to my father and there he was, big Max, all 17 ½ stone of him in overalls and with his nail bag on. And he put on the baggy green and there was a tear of pride for what his son had achieved. For my dream of playing on the Melbourne Cricket Ground was his dream as well. It is the most iconic piece I own and all the money in the world couldn't buy it.'

While Hughes controversially chose to lead a rebel Australian team in the old, iniquitous South Africa in the summers of 1985-86 and 1986-87 he always held dear, if silently, his deep affection for what he publicly terms 'our most powerful national emblem'.

'The baggy green sums up our country. It sums up the mateship; the Anzac spirit; the refusal to take a backward step. We may not win but at least we go down swinging,' observed Hughes, who played 70 Test matches between 1977 and 1984.

This is the tenor of the thesis he puts before audiences when he and former Australian football identity Ken Judge take their 'Captain and Coach' talkfest into the school classroom or business seminar.

He particularly enjoys speaking to schoolchildren and encouraging them to work hard and to believe their dreams can be fulfilled, their ambitions realised. He has vivid memories of his boyhood dream of wanting to wear the baggy green. 'My whole life was geared to it and around it. I had always known the baggy green was the highest honour you could get.'

It follows that he anticipates most children will ask to be photographed with the cap. So it was with some surprise that he greeted news at a school at Katanning, on the wheat belt 277km south-east of Perth, that widespread photography with the cap may not be appropriate. There was, a teacher confided, the possibility of nits. After explaining this dilemma to Judge and to teachers at another school in Katanning it was decided to risk the consequences and permit the customary photo call.

Late in the session a pupil insisted on having his photograph taken with Hughes. There was a proviso, however. Hughes had to wear the cap. He duly did so and to Judge's considerable amusement Hughes scratched his scalp all the way back to Perth. At that point the former Australian captain was pleased he had not brought to 'Show and Tell' the caps he had swapped with Viv Richards (West Indies), Mike Brearley (England) and Kapil Dev (India).

By no means are Walker and Hughes alone in their testaments to the power of the baggy green at a public presentation.

Frank Misson, the indefatigable NSW fast bowler who played five Tests against the West Indies and England in 1960-61, used his baggy green to generate funds for people with disabilities in the years when he donated his services to the sterling work of the Northcott Society. Corporate diners paid good money to be photographed with the cap.

Misson's one regret is that he did not have other caps which could have added further lustre to the event and generated more shackles for the society's coffers.

However, due to an oversight which continues to haunt him, caps he had swapped with Wes Hall (West Indies) and Brian Statham (England) had been poorly protected in a nook in his garage and consumed by moths and silverfish.

MC

5
COLLECTORS

THE term cricketania was first used in *London Society* in August 1862 relating to 'literature, sayings or gossip' about cricket.[1] In *The Cricketer Winter Annual 1921-22*, F.S. Ashley-Cooper wrote that 'the collection of "cricketania" has again come in vogue'. The Cricketania Society was founded in October 1929 with the aim of creating a register of collectors and collating a census of rare publications and cricketania. It folded in 1935 and no similar body existed in Britain until the formation of the Cricket Memorabilia Society in 1987.

In the preface to *The Wisden Book of Cricket Memorabilia*, the authors acknowledged that collecting was 'an arcane pursuit, dominated by a handful of collectors and part-time dealers, but the advent of regular sales by leading London auction houses in 1978 has brought it to a far wider audience and attracted a far wider range of materials on to the market'.[2]

The MCC Bicentenary auction of 1987 realised £320,000 (it is estimated that other auctions in the previous decade had realised only £680,000.) Overall some 11,000 lots had sold for an average of about £90 each. If 1978 saw the birth of serious collecting the MCC auction of 1987 took it to another level in terms of prices achieved.

In 2008 there were at least a dozen auction companies dealing in cricket memorabilia worldwide, and scores of dealers who primarily dealt in books but also in ephemera, clothing, bats and caps. Added to this were the private deals, the ubiquitous charity auctions and finally the massive online trading conducted via eBay. In total the market is worth millions of dollars a year. The new market of limited edition or manufactured cricket memorabilia, which was once confined to collectables such as port[3] and the occasional artwork,[4] is now a massive industry in Australia and to a lesser extent in Britain, although it is still growing there.

To many collectors, cricket caps are an important and desirable artefact. They are the pinnacle of a collection. For many Australians, the cap represents the ultimate in memorabilia of any sport. The chance to own an item which one usually can only earn, while a paradox, proves all too tempting for many collectors. Passionate collectors repeatedly say that they would never put on a baggy green, that this would be almost 'sacrilegious'. The cap owner in general values the notion of the exclusivity of the cap, and many understand that they are custodians rather than owners of a relic that should be cared for and passed on.

Most collectors have a love of the game and a knowledge of its history, ethos and traditions. Most are or have been players, coaches and administrators. The collecting of memorabilia is an expression of their passion for the game. Collecting is rarely a pragmatic pursuit based on the possibility of financial gain.

There are three types of cricket collectors:

First, those who played the game at the highest level and have an appreciation of its history and legacy. Initially their collections would have started with their own items then been augmented with swapped pieces. This continues to grow after retirement.

The second collector is a non-player who likes to associate himself with success. He is also a collector of limited-edition memorabilia and he (generally collectors are male) will surround himself with images of successful people. Often these collectors are well-educated high achievers.

The third type of collector is a student of history, who has an affection for the game and its traditions. His interest in collecting is an intertwining of this fascination for sport and history. Most of these are voracious readers and accumulators of facts and statistics.

*****

Reflecting the private interest in caps, the public collections are becoming more diverse and more numerous.

Discussions with private and public collectors suggest that a cap is the ultimate representation of a player and his career. The challenge that the State Library of South Australia set itself in the late 1980s to 'find' Bradman's cap is seen by some as the starting point of the cap's recent elevation. The library had an excellent collection of Bradman memorabilia and following renovations it had room to adorn the collection with a prized cap.

The best collection of baggy greens is held at the Melbourne Cricket Ground. These are part of the collection of the Melbourne Cricket Club, which has a separate museum, and the Australian Gallery of Sport and Olympic Museum, which was opened in 1984. This building was demolished for the latest ground redevelopment and these two collections will come under the umbrella of the National Sports Museum (NSM) which is part of the renovated stadium. The MCC has 12 caps. Its 10 match baggy greens are Bill Woodfull's 1928-29, Lindsay Hassett's 1948, Clarrie Grimmett's 1932-33, Keith Rigg's 1936-37, Leo O'Brien's 1936-37, Richie Benaud's 1958-59, Neil Harvey's 1961, Peter Burge's 1964, Greg Chappell's 1970s, and Rod Marsh's from 1982-83.

Adding relevance to the collection is the fact that the Cricket Hall of Fame, whose inductees are announced each year at the Allan Border Medal function, is an MCC initiative. Many of the caps in the collection belonged to inductees of the Hall of Fame. Some caps have been donated, others bought. They range chronologically from 1928-29 to the recent commemoratives of 2000 and 2001. All caps are important to the different museums, and each has a different story to tell in context with that museum's charter. The MCC collection is based on the social history of sport.[5] The Hall of Fame concentrates on the inductees and the NSM is dedicated to the display and interpretation of 20 sports, with emphasis on Olympic Games, Australian rules football and cricket.

The NSM was opened in March 2008. It contains a Baggy Green Room, which houses a majority of the cap collection. The NSM incorporates the Australian Cricket Hall of Fame, the Sport Australia Hall of Fame and the Olympic exhibition. The MCC oversees these various collections and their acquisitions policy is not based on emotion but relevance: such things as how the story of a particular cap relates to the ground, its members or cricket in general. The overriding factors are the cap's provenance, its condition and relevance.[6]

The Bradman Museum at Bowral has a number of the Don's caps, significantly the 1936-37 Test cap Sir Donald gave to the museum and a NSW cap which was purchased from the person who had been given the cap by Bradman in 1939.

The museum's curator, David Wells, explained the collection: 'The Bradman Museum seeks out caps for inclusion in its collection as we regard them as the most potent symbol of cricket achievement, regardless of the standard. Obviously the baggy green, with its long tradition as the pinnacle of Australian cricket, is the most desirable of all, but we collect other caps as well, as they also inform our knowledge of the game.'

Wells also noted that the baggy style is particular to cricket and that caps are valued by the players over any other cricket equipment. Wells said that caps tell us first and foremost which club or team a player represented and at what level. Dated baggy greens tell us during what Test series they were used. The cut of the baggy green tells us that Australia developed the confidence after WWI to establish a design more suited to our climate and to distance itself from mother England.

The State Library of South Australia's Mortlock Collection houses many items donated by Sir Donald Bradman, however it did not have a cap. The quest for Bradman caps has resulted in the library now displaying three of his baggy greens.

Sir Donald gave his 1928 cap to his neighbours, the Dunhams, in the 1950s. The cap loaned to the library by son Peter Dunham went on display when the collection was reopened by John Bradman in November 2003. Bradman gave his 1934 cap to Jack Bahan, a friend and golfing partner in the 1930s. His grandson David Brown loaned the library the cap which went on display in 1992.

Kevin Truscott gave the library the 1948 cap that Sir Donald had given to his father, Edgar. In his role as assistant manager at the London office of the Union Bank of Australia Edgar Truscott helped Bradman with his banking during the 1948 tour.[7] This cap was presented to the library at the SACA Test dinner in November 2004.

Private collectors show similar discretion and passion.

David Frith, the respected author and long-time collector, acquired his first baggy green in 1969. 'The first Australian Test cap I acquired was Ted McDonald's, and this was, I think, in 1969, in the north of England, in an antiques arcade. McDonald's 1921 cap, which is badly worn about the peak and has a few moth-holes, is English "skull cap" design. It is also quite small, but I understand that this is the result of the passing of the years; shrinkage is unavoidable. It was made by Rowan Glasgow (author's note: the UK manufacture explains the English shape). Grimmett's 1924-25 is faded but otherwise in good condition. It is slightly baggy in design. I bought the first three and was given the last two: McDonald, Clarrie Grimmett (1924-25), Gil Langley (1953), Jeff Thomson (1977) and Allan Border (1989).[8]

Why does Frith collect baggy greens? 'They are particularly significant items in my large collection of memorabilia,' he

Invincible … Neil Harvey, generally bareheaded at the crease or in the field, gave away all but one of his caps including this one for the 1949-50 tour of South Africa. The exception was the cap he wore on the Invincibles tour of England in 1948.
Photo: courtesy Ern McQuillan

said. Given that his collection comprises thousands of pieces this is a significant statement about the cap's status.

Frith noted changes in attitudes towards collecting baggy greens since 1969: 'They simply weren't to be found in those days, except in the rare instance when one might have been presented to a museum. There were no cricket auctions until the late 1970s. Gradually former cricketers have overcome reluctance to part with the caps; they fetch big money, and some have several of them, so why not? Of all a Test cricketer's attire, surely the cap is the most significant, treasured above all other items of clothing?'

Sydney collector John Kirkness, who was featured in *The Sydney Morning Herald's* Money supplement,[9] said: 'When a kid dreams of playing for his country he dreams of a baggy green, not a floppy hat or Test shirts adorned with logo, initials and Test number.'

Kirkness believes the refusal by CA to sell replicas is important. 'Cricket is unique in Australia and you cannot buy a replica cap, as you can with jerseys for other national teams such as the Kangaroos, Wallabies and Socceroos. A baggy green is desirable, irrespective of who played in it. Certainly a cap is more valuable depending on the player but there is definite kudos with a cap before you add the player's additional charisma. I did like it when the series was listed on the cap; in that way you could directly relate the events of a series with a player – there was a historical link.'

With dates no longer printed on caps Kirkness would like to see the player number on the cap as is done with England caps and the Australian ODI caps.

Kirkness owns one baggy green cap and several Australian helmets. He also collects NSW caps, as they too have rarely changed. (Author's note: apparently there have been only two badges worn on NSW caps since the middle part of the 19th century.) This, Kirkness says, adds to the NSW cap's significance and desirability. 'All the other states have changed their caps and emblem; some many times over.'

Brisbane collector Harry Wszola, who has a full-size cap and one of the miniature presentation caps, believes that the heritage of Australian sport should be preserved through collecting. As well as cricket, he collects memorabilia from many sports. His motivation is to ensure that his children and their descendants appreciate the sportsmen of the past, understanding the sacrifices many made to reach the top. Wszola shelved his sporting career for academic studies and relates to the struggle of those who excelled in the amateur era and received little monetary compensation (if any) for their endeavours. Wszola does not consider the monetary value of the caps, as he does not buy them for resale. The same rule will apply for his descendants when it is their turn to be the custodians of the caps.

MF

References

1 *Sporting Traditions*, May 1994 – Peter Sharpham.
2 'Branding of Australian Cricket: Culture, Commerce, Cricket and the baggy green cap', *Sporting Traditions*, November 2006 – Richard Cashman.
3 *The Pictorial History of Australian Cricket* – Jack Pollard, J.M. Dent 1983.
4 Ibid.
5 *The Demon Spofforth* – Richard Cashman, UNSWP, 1990.
6 'The Green and Gold – 100 Years Young', *Wisden Cricketers' Almanack Australia* 1999 – Philip Derriman.
7 *Pageant of Cricket* – David Frith, Macmillan, 1987.
8 *Glorious Innings – Treasures from the Melbourne Cricket Club Collection* – Richard Bouwman, Hutchinson Australia 1987.
9 Pollard, op. cit.
10 Newspaper cutting, NSWCA Library.
11 *History of the Melbourne Cricket Club* – Hugh Field, unpublished manuscript, MCC Library.

— STRANGE JOURNEYS —

Some of cricket's truest and tallest tales are told and retold on the deck of Barry Jarman's houseboat, be it moored at Lyrup or Loxton on the River Murray in South Australia.

Jarman, Australia's 33rd captain, is a generous host and for years his houseboat, *Gooda's Gold,* has provided a splendid retreat for many luminaries of South Australian and international cricket. Old flannels have much to recall and recount, and for years a special time for Jarman and his wife Gaynor was the annual visit of the late Norm O'Neill and his wife, Gwen, and Lindsay and Stella Kline.

Although Jarman, O'Neill and Kline played just one Test together — the 119-run defeat to India and its contentious off-spinner Jasu Patel at Kanpur the week before Christmas 1959 — their friendships had formed during a tour of New Zealand with the Second Australian XI under Ian Craig in 1956-57. And by the end of the arduous 12-week, eight-Test tour of Pakistan and India in 1959-60 they were sworn mates for life.

Their story-telling gathered richness with the passing summers. When conversation one lengthy happy hour on the houseboat turned to the baggy green, Jarman and Kline were distressed to realise O'Neill no longer had a cap in his possession.

Other than sympathising with his pal at the extent of his loss and disappointment Jarman said little. He knew, however, where he could locate a cap for O'Neill. Furthermore, it was one that O'Neill had worn during a 42-Test career that earned him a scrapbook brimful of rave reviews.

Before the exaltation of the baggy green it was not uncommon for players to swap caps with a teammate. Invariably players found cap sizes varied and often a colleague offered a cap which fitted more comfortably.

Among others, no doubt, this was the case for Neil Harvey and Colin McDonald, Bill Lawry and Frank Misson, Graham McKenzie and Ashley Mallett, and O'Neill and Jarman. And there is anecdotal evidence of Don Bradman and Keith Miller swapping caps in 1948.

For the majority of his distinguished 14-year first-class career with South Australia which saw him elevated for 19 Test matches, Jarman ran a successful sports store in Adelaide.

In 1962 as a favour to a friend, Ray Reece, the then chairman of the South Australian Trotting Club, Jarman employed Ray's son

Barry to undertake tasks that were within his reach at the shop and to run errands throughout the city. When he learnt Reece hero-worshipped Miller Jarman promptly nicknamed him 'Nugget'.

In no time at all 'Nugget' Reece became a well-known and much-loved identity in Adelaide and in 2008 remained a familiar figure in the dressingroom of the South Australian and Australian cricket teams and the Port Power Australian football club. Such is his unique relationship with the luminaries of Australian cricket that he was chosen as a subject for ABC televison's popular *Australian Story* program in 2006.

'Nugget', an unabashed devotee of Steve Waugh, Darren Lehmann and Jason Gillespie in particular, has been dined by Test cricketers and, indeed, photographed with them wearing the baggy green given to him by Jarman. But it was O'Neill's and not Jarman's name written inside the cap.

Faithfully promising 'Nugget' he would replace the cap with one bearing his name, Jarman in 2006 took the cap back to the houseboat and following the arrival of the Klines made a surprise presentation of it to O'Neill. The celebrated batsman, who was blighted throughout his career by erroneous and pointless comparisons with a young Don Bradman, was greatly moved.

After a celebratory drink O'Neill regaled his friends with the tale of a NSW player who years earlier had returned to Sydney and told him: 'I couldn't believe it but there was a bloke in Adelaide with your Australian cap.' The bloke was 'Nugget' Reece.

Jarman was understudy to Wally Grout throughout his career and often there were long periods when he was not required for Test duty. He made his debut at Kanpur and left international cricket a decade later against the West Indies in Adelaide. Just six months earlier, in July 1968, he had the privilege of captaining Australia in the absence of the injured Bill Lawry for the drawn fourth Test with England at Headingley, Leeds.

Jarman played 12 of his 19 Tests with Ian Redpath who had an outstanding career of 66 Tests from January 1964 to February 1976.

Early in his international career Redpath gave his first baggy green cap to Ted Davies, his coach at The Geelong College for whom he had great admiration and affection. At times he thought wistfully about the cap and was stunned in 2005 when the ex-wife of the late Davies's deceased son, presented the cap to Cricket Victoria asking that it be returned to Redpath.

In semi-retirement and turning his hand to painting watercolours and playing golf, Redpath smiles at the recollection of being reunited with the cap so thoughtfully mounted and boxed by a forever grateful Cricket Victoria. It takes pride of place among his cricket possessions.

'As one gets older I think you look back at the significance of the baggy green. It is, after all, looked upon with reverence by the community,' said Redpath.

MC

Reunited ... Norm and Gwen O'Neill with the well-travelled baggy green aboard Barry Jarman's houseboat on the River Murray in South Australia. O'Neill died in March 2008, aged 71.
Photo: courtesy Barry Jarman

— ONE TEST IN TIME —

At the end of the summer of 2007-08 the number of players to have made a solitary appearance in the baggy green cap stood at 62.

Indisputably some were unfortunate not to have played more often, circumstances conspiring against them at the most critical moment of their career. Conversely, others were fortunate to have had their 30 hours of fame. Invariably matters of selection are complex and often emotive. As is the case in the middle, generally it is all about timing.

Certainly Nathan Hauritz, Dan Cullen and Chris Rogers, ambitious young men, remain hopeful they will be given another opportunity to wear their baggy green caps.

As the powerbrokers of Cricket Australia and the Australian Cricketers' Association found more common ground in the late 1990s and into the new millennium they pooled resources to formally recognise and celebrate the accomplishments of the country's elite cricketers at various ceremonies and functions.

Opening batsman Ken Eastwood, who made his one appearance when Australia lost the Ashes at Sydney in February 1971, is as humbled as he is delighted to walk with men whose names are familiar in households throughout the land and beyond.

In his mind, at least, the egalitarianism of Australian cricket is celebrated whenever and wherever there is a gathering of men who have worn the baggy green.

'Whether you played one Test or 100 you are part of a group and always treated as an equal,' said Eastwood. 'I'm proud to be a member of such an elite group. It was a bonus as far as I am concerned. It is surprising what one Test can do for you. I am invited to various functions and dinners.'

A remarkable sequence of events led to Eastwood's selection at the age of 35, a season after he had been feted as Victoria's highest run-scorer (744 runs at 41.33) while Bill Lawry's Australian team were on their torturous tour of India and South Africa.

As Lawry, Keith Stackpole, Paul Sheahan and Ian Redpath were ahead of him in the pecking order Eastwood never realistically expected to be summoned by the national selectors.

It may have been a home Test match but Eastwood is the owner of two baggy greens which in all probability will be bequeathed to his daughters, Jennifer and Catherine. He was given a choice of caps but officials it seems were so distracted following the controversial sacking of Lawry as captain and player that no effort was made to reclaim the one he rejected.

Peter Allan and Ashley Woodcock each have three caps to show for their one outing in the baggy green. Allan received two for his selection in Bob Simpson's team for the famously acrimonious tour of the West Indies in 1964-65 and a third when chosen for his one appearance, against England at the Gabba in December 1965 when Doug Walters announced his genius with 155 on debut.

Woodcock, who from a very young age intuitively understood that the baggy green epitomised the pinnacle for a cricketer, was presented with his first cap when chosen to open the batting against a World XI in 1971-72 following the cancellation of a scheduled tour by South Africa because of the threat of disruption by anti-apartheid protesters. Two years later he made his debut against New Zealand in front of his supportive home crowd at Adelaide Oval and then toured New Zealand. However he did not perform well enough in the minor matches to dislodge either Redpath or Stackpole who was at the end of a most entertaining 43-Test career.

Leg-spinner Rex Sellers, who successfully reinvented himself as a batsman for South Australia, retired from the first-class game in 1967 just months before Woodcock, a lean and elegant stroke player, made his first-class debut.

Sellers, who was born at the tiny siding of Balsar about 100 kilometres north of Mumbai where his father was based as an engineer and bridge inspector in the Indian railways, had the satisfaction of making his only appearance at Kolkata in October 1964.

Although rain ruined the match, his selection provided some compensation for the frustration of missing so much of the preceding England tour because of surgery to his spinning finger.

The egalitarianism of which Eastwood is so proud is echoed by Kim Hughes, Australia's 37th captain, and a thrilling batsman who polarised the Australian cricket community when for two tumultuous summers he forsook the baggy green and played in rebel colours in South Africa.

'It is noticeable at big reunions of past players that there is no pecking order. If you have the baggy green you are on the team whether you have played one Test or 50. I'm very proud of that,' said Hughes.

Despite the turbulence of the time only once in 28 Tests as Australian captain did Hughes lead a player chosen only once for his country. In his first match as captain deputising for the injured Graham Yallop in the second Test with Pakistan at Perth in March 1979, he oversaw the debut of Yallop's replacement, Victorian Jeff Moss.

Such was the acrimony of proceedings it was soon forgotten that Australia prospered by seven wickets and that Moss made a useful contribution to the victory.

That Pakistani paceman Sikander Bakht was run out by the bowler Alan Hurst while backing up and Andrew Hilditch was given out handled the ball after retrieving a wayward return and handing the ball to prickly Sarfraz Nawaz obscured the fact that Moss scored 22 and an undefeated 38 to win some encouraging notices.

With Allan Border, Moss added 81 in an unbroken fourth wicket partnership and had the satisfaction of leg glancing guileful medium-pacer Mudassar Nazar for the single which enabled the Australians to square the two-match contest after they lost heavily in the opening Test in Melbourne.

Moss appeared in one match at the 1979 World Cup in England but was not chosen for the Test tour of India under Hughes later in the year and did not again play for Australia.

Be that as it may, Hughes tips his cap to Moss who rejoices at being treated as one of the family whenever those privileged to have worn the baggy green gather to talk of their days in the sun.

MC

6
VALUES

THE idea of a baggy green having monetary value is only a recent phenomenon.

Before the first sports auction held by Phillips in London in 1978, caps were generally not bought and sold but swapped or given away. They might reappear in a flea market or antiques store. Caps had great value to players because they had to earn them with good performances but they had no monetary value as no market existed for sports memorabilia. The rise of sports auctions, websites and electronic auctions has meant that a market for caps has grown substantially.

Over the past 16 years, there have been 168 offerings of baggy greens for sale. There is reliable data for 122 sales while the rest were passed in or sold privately after the auction. This information comes mainly from the major auction houses, sports specialists, with some sales figures from retailers and charity events.

The total value of those 122 sales is $2,089,037 (all financial figures are in Australian dollars unless otherwise specified). After excluding one cap sold at a testimonial and donated back, the average of these sales is $16,893 a cap. The five Bradman caps, which averaged almost $160,000 a sale, have attracted much higher prices than other caps so we will exclude them from this calculation. Bradman caps aside, baggy greens have sold for an average price of $10,753. An alternative measure is the median amount paid; again excluding Bradman caps, this is a more modest $7500.

The major dealers in baggy greens are Charles Leski in Melbourne, (who have offered 48 caps) Christies Australia (28) and Ludgroves (20), while Knights Auctions in Britain have sold 27. Others in Australia are Lawsons (6), Sports Memorabilia Australia/Legends Genuine Memorabilia (14), Icons of Sports (2), Framous and Bonham & Goodman's (3). In Britain, Graham Budd Auctions (2), Mullock Madeley Auctions (2), Bonham & Brooks (1) and T. Vennett-Smith Auctions (2).

It should be pointed out that most of these sales were conducted at public auctions. Auction prices will traditionally be lower than those achieved by retail. A Brisbane memorabilia retailer has sold six caps over the past five years and their retail prices were higher than the auction-based information in the table. The cap of a modestly performed Test player generally retails for between $10,000 and $15,000, while the cap of a high-profile name can command $20,000-$30,000. These amounts are for caps that have been expertly mounted and presented.

What have been some of the highlights over the years? In ascending order, the record prices achieved chronologically have been (including the Trumper and Bradman caps):

Sale year	Player and Series Year	Other	Trumper	Bradman
1988	Grimmett 1932-33	$1,200		
1995	Bradman 1946-47 (1)			$7,500
1997	Walters 1974	$4,232		
1997	Trumper 1899		$28,750	
1998	Grimmett 1930	$7,475		
1999	Woodfull 1932-33	$23,000		
2000	Oldfield 1932-33	$28,000		
2002	Miller 1953	$35,250		
2003	Bradman 1947-48			$180,000
2003	Bradman 1946-47 (2)			$88,835
2003	Bradman 1948			$425,000
2004	Trumper 1907		$83,000	
2004	Bradman 1930			$95,385
2005	Morris 1948	$40,000		
2005	Bradman 1946-47 (1)			$95,400
2006	Miller 1954-55	$40,775		

The big names – Bradman, Trumper and Miller – and the big series – 1932-33 and 1948 – command the highest prices.

Another way to compare price increases over time is to compare the amount realised when the same cap has appeared a number of times. For example, Colin McDonald's 1956 cap sold at Leski's in 1999 for $2990 then at Knights in 2002 for $6571 and again at Knights in 2005 for $7896. This represents a 264 per cent increase in six years. Wally Grout's 1962-63 cap sold at Phillips in 2000 for $7200 and at Leski's four years later for $31,455, a 436 per cent increase. Don Tallon's 1950-51 cap sold at Ludgrove's in 2003 for $7000 then two years later at Leski's for $12,815, a 183 per cent increase.

How do baggy green prices compare to similar items such as helmets and ODI caps? Only 11 ODI caps have sold in the same period for an average price of $1850. The World Series Cricket (WSC) caps worn in Supertests and one-day matches have fared a little better, averaging $2750 for the four sold.

There have been 14 Australian blazers sold at an average price of $2990. The best price achieved was $8225 for Keith Miller's 1953 tour blazer. Test sweaters average $745 from nine sales, and Test shirts an average of $1500 from four sales.

Helmets, green and yellow, have attracted less interest. Twelve have been offered with estimates ranging from $600 for Ray Bright's to $5000 for Mark Waugh's, but there have been no sales apart from the auction of a significant helmet worn by Steve Waugh when he made 200 in the West Indies in 1995. The helmet was signed by the squad and offered with signed batting gloves used in the innings. It sold for $11,500.

Clearly, the baggy green has commanded a significant premium over other items of cricket apparel.

The prices for the variations on the baggy green design are interesting. Three baggy whites (1988 Bicentennial Test) have sold for an average of $4075; a

2000 player's Millennium cap for $15,000 and a 2003 presentation miniature for $5000.

*****

What are the trends and the implications for the market in the future? From 2004 to 2007, the average price per cap was $16,170; from 1997 to 2003 it was $8215. So caps have doubled in value in 10 years.

What does this tell us? In basic terms the values are increasing, but they depend on the player whose baggy green is being sold, the year and series, and the condition of the cap.

The passing of time plays a role. Trumper's first cap, from the important 1899 series, sold for $28,750 in 1997. The next, from 1907, went for $83,000 in 2004. Speculation about what the 1899 cap might achieve in today's market suggests a minimum of $100,000.

Keith Miller's caps have also grown in value. In 1999 his 1952-53 cap sold for $8700. In 2002 his 1953 cap brought $35,200; in 2006 his 1954-55 baggy went for $40,775 and his 1956 one for $29,125. The last cap had minor wear holes in the brim.

Miller had a great series against the West Indies in 1954-55 – 20 wickets and 439 runs – and this was reflected in the price achieved for that cap.

Many people lament the sale of caps, believing that an item earned or given as a gift should not be sold. These are reasonable reservations but a market cannot be prohibited. Some ethics can coexist with the sale of caps. Some recipients (or their children) have returned caps to the cricketer or his descendants. In one case a player had given the cap away years before and now a descendant of the original beneficiary wished to sell it. The dealer, feeling uneasy that a gift was being profited from, ensured that the player received a cut from his commission of the sale.

What motivates a person to buy a cap? A collector may wish to have one from a certain series, or it may have belonged to a favourite player. The motivation is different for each and hence predicting the result of individual sales is difficult, as it depends on who is looking to buy at the time.

Some caps were not included in this analysis. The Bradman caps, which are dealt with later, were excluded because of the huge prices they have attracted. Another excluded belonged to Greg Matthews. This was auctioned at a testimonial organised by his manager Max Markson in December 1998. The cap was sold for $45,000 and was returned to Matthews by the bidder, Carl Howell, the head of Advanced Hair Studios, for whom Matthews was an advertising star.[1] The price was vastly more than expected, which can't be fully explained by the charity element of the auction. Research revealed that from sale proceeds of more than $200,000 at the function, $10,000 was donated to charity.

Of more interest than the tax-free payment that Matthews received from the auction, was the question posed by Philip Koch, a journalist from *The Sunday Telegraph*. He suggested that the sale by Matthews had caused consternation but acknowledged that the recent sale of Olympic and Commonwealth Games medals won by Betty Cuthbert, Raelene Boyle and Dawn Fraser in the period 1996-1998, while unusual for sport, was just catching up with the long-established trade in bravery medals, including Victoria Crosses. The sale of the Michael Whitney cap in 1993 was cited as the only other recent sale of a baggy green.

Reacting to the Matthews sale Steve Waugh said: 'I don't consider my cap to be memorabilia. It's something to treasure. It will be passed on to my family.'[2]

Matthews expected criticism for selling his cap. 'If there's "x" amount of people out there having difficulty comprehending where I'm coming from, I apologise for that,' he said. 'But Greg Matthews is 100 per cent happy within himself.'[3]

Where do prices go from here? Research and experience confirm that most collectors are cricket lovers. Large speculative investment has not arrived. There is potential for this to develop, especially with as prestigious an item as the baggy green. Some reasons for this potential include: an increase in the knowledge of how many caps are out there and who has them; increased availability of funds due to superannuation; the interest shown by five major collecting institutions in Australia; and reduced supply, given that since the mid-1990s players have been limited to one cap.

The examples of world soccer and US baseball memorabilia might seem stratospheric but what is to stop speculative investors becoming interested in cricket memorabilia? In 2002 Pele's 1970 Brazilian World Cup shirt sold for £157,750 and Sir Geoff Hurst's 1966 England World Cup shirt reached $263,120. The bat Sir Garfield Sobers used to hit the record six sixes in an over at Cardiff in 1968 sold at Christies for $146,875, and Shane Gould's 1972 Munich Olympics diary was bought for $41,125 by the NSW State Library.

Honus Wagner, the Pittsburgh Pirates shortstop who played around the turn of the 20th century, had a cigarette card featuring him withdrawn from distribution because he opposed smoking. This extremely rare card has sold for as much as $US1.265 million. In February 2007 it achieved $US2.35m and only six months later $US2.8m.[4] Recent legal cases over baseballs hit for home run records have highlighted the extremes people will go to because of the money involved. Mark McGwire's 1998 record-breaking 70th season home run ball sold for $US3.2 million while in 2003 the 73rd season home run ball of Barry Bonds sold for $US450,000.

Given the increased prices achieved recently and the increasing age of many caps, prices for baggy greens should rise, especially for caps from great players or from famous

Among the elite ... some of the most sought after baggy greens are those once worn by Australia's 42 Test captains. Allan Border, the 38th skipper, led his side in a world record 93 Test matches. **Photo: unknown**

series – 1920-21, Bodyline 1932-33, the Invincibles in 1948 and the team's run of 16 consecutive Test wins to March 2001 and a further 16 successive victories to January 2008.

Only 18 caps dating from before 1940 have been sold publicly in the past 20 years. Others may have been held in private collections and been sold privately. Significantly, 15 of these were sold before 2003. Prices have doubled since. The average for caps form the pre-1940 era is $16,447. These are probably worth double that amount today. Only five caps from before 1930 have been sold. They are rare indeed.

MF

References

1 *The Sunday Telegraph*, 6/12/98 – 'Past for Sale' – Philip Koch.
2 ibid.
3 *The Australian*, 5/12/98.
4 http://www.scpauctions.com/wagner_press_release.htm

— CAP BURGLARS —

The baggy green had a mystique and an allure long before it was endowed with the iconic status of a national symbol.

But since it has been aggressively sought by collectors and investors and commands tens of thousands of dollars at auction the cap needs to be protected with greater vigilance.

Ricky Ponting, Michael Kasprowicz and Jason Gillespie each had a cap stolen as the romanticising of the baggy green intensified and its commercial value increased during the 1990s. Graham McKenzie, among others, had a cap purloined when less thought was given to its significance and value. Mind you, this did not lessen the sense of loss or quell the anger at the time.

Rarely, of course, does the aggrieved player learn the identity of the culprit. Only a successful police investigation or an admission of guilt and offer of restitution by the offender can provide some solace.

To his despair, the laconic and affable off-spinner and gully specialist Ashley 'Rowdy' Mallett had two caps stolen in extraordinary circumstances during his 38-Test career.

The extent to which someone will go to steal a baggy green was graphically illustrated to Mallett when he was 12th man at a major match for charity in 1974-75.

On this occasion his duties extended beyond the dressing room and he moved among the spectators at the MCG to collect donations for the victims of Cyclone Tracy which devastated Darwin on Christmas Day 1974, claiming 50 lives on land and 16 at sea.

As he rattled the tin for the cause a villain in a group which had surrounded him deftly removed the cap from his hip pocket and disappeared into the mob. Mallett knows nothing of its fate or whether it ever reached the memorabilia market in Australia or England.

However, an extraordinary letter from a member of the English establishment in November 1998 provided the definitive explanation for the disappearance of his England tour cap stolen from the MCC members' changing room at Lord's in 1972.

Richard Robins, the godson of Don Bradman and a recipient of a baggy green from the game's greatest batsman, confessed to nicking Mallett's cap after a pre-season practice session with his mates at the Nursery at Lord's.

Robins wrote: 'In 1972 when you toured with the Australian side, your team used the members' changing room in which to leave all their kit and I am afraid that many of us young MCC players used to try on the baggy green caps which were lying around the changing area. I tried yours on and it fitted extremely well! To my great shame, I kept it (leaving an Eton Ramblers cricket cap in its place).'

The son of the late Walter Robins, who played 19 Tests for England between 1929 and 1937 and chaired the national selection panel in the 1960s, Robins thought little if at all about the cap until 1998 when his mother discovered what the moths had abandoned at the back of the airing cupboard in the family home in Suffolk.

To assuage his guilt Robins had it elaborately and expensively repaired by reputable antique fabric restorers in the Midlands and in time apologetically showed it to Mallett over lunch in Adelaide.

Delighted that it had not perished and that Robins finally honoured his promise of the Eton Ramblers cap which was nowhere to be found in 1972, Mallett magnanimously permitted Robins to keep the baggy green. But, when he later asked for it to be returned so he could present it to the Ayr Cricket Club in Scotland with which he had such a happy association in his playing days, Mallett was shocked to learn Robins had sold it for an unknown sum.

Mallett has no idea what the cap would have fetched at auction but with a wry smile concedes it would be many tens of thousands of dollars shy of the $425,000 Robins received from the sale of the cap Bradman gave him in 1956. At the time Bradman had returned to England to cover the Ashes for *The Daily Mail.*

Bradman was particularly close to Walter Robins and recuperated at his home at Burnham, Essex, after sustaining a flake fracture of his right ankle in the final Test at The Oval in August 1938.

Such was their association that 10 years later Robins acted as the Australian Board of Control's liaison officer for Bradman's Invincibles tour. Robins, who captained England against New Zealand in 1937, died in 1968 at the age of 62.

While Mallett gave away other caps three remain in a South Australian bank vault to bequeath to his son Ben.

In his final match, the Centenary Test of 1980 at Lord's, Mallett was the only player wearing a cap bearing a date. Given that from the age of six he had dreamed of earning a baggy green, he thought it appropriate he should wear the cap given him for his first Test, also against England at The Oval in 1968.

For 19 of his 38 Test matches between 1968 and 1980 Mallett was captained by the redoubtable Ian Chappell who, while steeped in the history of the game, has great respect but no particular affection for the cap. Indeed, he is troubled by what he considers the ostentatious displays of the baggy green which have become increasingly fashionable over the past 10 years or so. He has no emotional attachment to the cap and, unlike his brother Greg, does not have one among his possessions. Nor, he says, does he know the whereabouts of any of them.

Indeed, it took Mallett to tell Chappell, his mentor and friend, that one of his caps was conspicuously presented, with those donated by Greg Chappell and Graeme Hole, in a showcase at the Glenelg Cricket Club in Adelaide where he had launched his career.

Coincidentally, it is another set of stairs an ocean away which provides Chappell with a rare and specific recollection of one of his baggy greens.

In February 1970 he was trudging up the stairs to the dressing room at the bloodhouse that can be the Bullring at the Wanderers in Johannesburg, angry at being bowled for a duck by hardnosed Eddie Barlow. A moment later he was seething when a spectator snatched his cap.

'As I hit the stairs some bastard took it off the top of my head,' said Chappell. And from that day forth he removed his cap as he made his way back to the pavilion.

There is an amusing sequel to this tale.

'A couple of years ago in Perth I went to dinner at the home of a mate of mine, Simon Davies, who I met in Rhodesia (now Zimbabwe) at the start of the South African tour in 1966-67,' recounted Chappell.

'Another guy from Zimbabwe was there and he said: "I've got a cap of yours." I said: "You're not the bastard who took it off my head?" And he replied: "No, but I might have bought it from the bloke who did!"'

MC

7
THE ULTIMATE BAGGY GREEN

DON Bradman bestrode the game like a colossus. He set numerous records, affected the game's laws and history, and even influenced the way memorabilia is collected.

An examination of Bradman's Test caps – what he did with them, where they ended up, how they have been marketed and the prices they attract at auction – provides a wonderful snapshot of the baggy green market. This saga includes auctioneers, media corporations, the prime minister and his Goods & Services Tax (GST)[1], museums, valuers, wealthy buyers, lucky sellers, perceptive investors and generous individuals.

When discussion turns to memorabilia, especially baggy green caps, the main question always is: 'What is it worth?' The mainstream press has a fascination with the dollar value of caps and the increase in these prices over the years. This is understandable as it is an easy way to measure interest. However price is not always an indication of an item's value or desirability. Many artefacts from cricket's so-called Golden Age, from the 1890s to 1915, appeal to only a small selection of enthusiasts. The general public has fleeting knowledge of the players from this period and, apart from the giants of that era, W.G. Grace and Victor Trumper, there is not a great deal of public interest in its history and memorabilia.

Sir Donald Bradman's legacy transcends his unsurpassed record as a player, administrator and selector. As well, his fame has fired the public's interest in cricket and cricketers from the 1920s. His eminence and longevity have ensured that many tens of thousands of cricket fans have read and continue to read about his life and the cricketers entwined in it. In doing so, the general public is familiar with cricket events of 75 years ago. In Australia this depth of knowledge does not occur in other sports, probably not even in politics or general history. Unwitting participants in Bradman's career are known half a world and half a century away: England's Eric Hollies, with a modest Test career, is almost as well known in Australia as Test hero Harold Larwood and his Bodyline captain, Douglas Jardine. Most Australians could not name the national rugby union or rugby league captains from the 1930s let alone those from Britain.

Even Bradman's recollections of cricket in his youth are a powerful statement on the game. His praise of Charlie Macartney's innings of 170 at the SCG in 1921, the first Test the then 12-year-old Bradman had attended, was influential in the campaign to have Macartney inducted into the Cricket Australia Hall of Fame in 2007.

The growth of the memorabilia industry, the continued interest, or obsession, some would argue, with Sir Donald Bradman and the revaluation of the baggy green's legacy were reflected in the 2003 marketing, auction and sale of Bradman's 1946-47 and 1948 baggy greens.

The near deification of Bradman was espoused by former prime minister John Howard: 'So he was more than just a great cricketer and great sportsman, he was a dominant Australian personality in a way which I don't think any other person has been in the last 100 years. Sir Donald Bradman's contribution was more than to the game of cricket. It was his role in the history and development of Australia that will also be remembered. No individual has so inspired successive generations of Australians across such a breadth of age, geography and circumstances as Sir Donald.'[2]

The outpouring of public grief at Bradman's passing in 2001 enabled a remarkable marketing campaign to be orchestrated – all centred on a Bradman cap. With the baggy green now so high in the public's esteem, several caps were marketed by former Christie's Australia auctioneer, Michael Ludgrove, and former Australian Cricket Board CEO, Graham Halbish, who had formed the short-lived but headline-grabbing auction house, Ludgrove's. Two Bradman caps would smash records, cause a certain amount of intrigue and gain international attention. Yet both never went under the hammer.

In 2003, News Ltd, in conjunction with Ludgrove's, launched a public appeal in its nationwide stable of newspapers. The aim, as proclaimed on the front pages, was to 'Bring the 1948 baggy green home'. With an obvious nationalist pitch, an appeal for $500,000 was launched – the price of a substantial family home, just for a cricket cap. This appeal attracted a pledge of financial support from CA[3] and generated huge publicity for the proposed auction, which was to be held by Ludgrove's in London in June 2003.

Was $500,000 unreasonable? The only way to answer that is to examine other Bradman caps in museums and their history at auction. From 1995 to 2003 collectors witnessed an increase in the reported sale price of a Bradman cap.

According to *The Wisden Book of Cricket Memorabilia*, the big auction houses began to specialise in cricket memorabilia in 1978. Then came the 1987 MCC Bicentennial auction, a blockbuster that set numerous records. Not long after the birth of large auctioning of cricket memorabilia the first Bradman cap was put up for sale. On 22 September, 1995 Christie's at South Kensington, London offered his 1946-47 cap. It was listed simply as: 'BRADMAN, Sir Donald George – An Australian cap in green embroidered with the Australian crest and legends "Australia. 1946-47", with a card stapled to the brim inscribed in Bradman's hand: "To Tim Biles. From

Don Bradman" (torn and creased) PROVENANCE: The Revd. Canon Timothy Biles – see footnote to lot 87).'

The estimate was £300-500 and this was well and truly shattered with a final bid of £3375 ($7800 at the time). This cap, the Biles 1946-47 cap, (the need for a distinction over and above the year will be explained later) was bought by a West Australian school teacher, Cameron Tingley.

Only two other Bradman caps were in the public domain at the time, and both had been given away by Sir Donald. His 1934 cap was on loan to the State Library of South Australia. He had given it to Jack Bahen, a friend and golfing partner in the late 1930s. Bahen's grandson, David Brown, gave the cap to the library for a long-term loan and it was displayed briefly in 1992. The other cap was Sir Donald's 1936-37 baggy green, which he had donated to the Bradman Museum in 1993.

No other Bradman caps emerged for another eight years, then, in a 21-month period to November 2004, another six caps were offered at Christie's and Ludgrove's, or loaned to the State Library of South Australia.

To date, there are nine Bradman caps in the public domain and each one's journey from Sir Donald to the current owner provides an interesting story. There may be others which have been in private hands and only a select few know of their existence. How many are there? This is a difficult question, given that players were often issued with two caps per tour. The existence of two caps per player from the 1946-47 series and the possibility that this happened in other home series means there might be more Bradman baggy greens than historians and experts have estimated. The swapping of caps among teammates has clouded the quest to locate every Bradman baggy. Time may reveal the correct number as more caps are unearthed and original contracts show how many caps each player received.

The first of the six new Bradman baggies to surface was from the 1947-48 series against India in Australia. Ludgrove's offered it at an auction in Melbourne in February 2003. In stark contrast to the paucity of description for the first cap auctioned, the 1946-47 cap at Christie's in 1995, this auction's catalogue information ran to three pages with four photographs. Yet little information about the provenance of the cap was published, although the catalogue said that a 'detailed letter of provenance signed by the vendor is available'. Estimates of between $100,000 and $200,000 were a huge increase over the previous public auction amount of $7800 achieved eight years earlier.

Ludgrove's publicity saw pre-auction reports in News Limited's *The Sunday Telegraph* and *The Australian*. These papers announced expectations of $500,000 and between

The greatest team … Bradman's 1948 Ashes tourists are still considered Australia's greatest team. Here Bradman, far left, leads his team onto the field during the 1948 tour. Also from left: Lindsay Hassett, Ernie Toshack, Colin McCool and Arthur Morris. **Photo: Ronald Cardwell**

$200,000 and $250,000 respectively. However the cap did not reach auction but, according to Ludgrove's, was sold by private treaty before the auction. The amount was not disclosed because of a confidentiality clause. The auction house did suggest that it was more than $180,000, the previous record for a Bradman item – a life-size statue.

With such an increase, surely this record would stand for years. That was not to be, as Ludgrove's then began its campaign to sell the 'Holy Grail' – Bradman's 1948 Invincibles cap. Here was the last Test cap worn by the game's greatest player on the only undefeated Ashes tour by an Australian team.

On May 21, 2003 all major News Ltd papers began a front-page 'quest to reclaim an Australian treasure' that was to be auctioned by Ludgrove's in Britain in July. One paper declared: '*The Daily Telegraph* is determined that cricket's most famous cap should be returned to Australia and displayed for posterity.'

The number of a bank account was listed and the public were invited to donate to the appeal. The vendor, Richard Robins, Sir Donald's godson, then offered the newspaper's Australian appeal an exclusive option to buy before auction; expectations were for a price of more than $500,000. The ACB pledged to donate $10,000 to the fund and many great names endorsed the appeal. As reported on the ABC television program *Media Watch*, Ricky Ponting, Keith Stackpole, Allan Border, Sir Donald's son, John Bradman, Merv Hughes and even Bali bomb victim Jason McCartney, the AFL player, supported the appeal. McCartney was quoted in *The Mercury* as saying: 'The cap definitely should come back home. It is a unique piece of Australian history.'

A lone dissenting voice was the Australian Test captain, Steve Waugh. 'To me, there are more important causes to raise money for,' he said after discussing with *The Sydney Morning Herald* his involvement in charity work in India.

Three weeks of choreographed appeals met with limited success and on 11 June, 2003 the *Herald Sun*, *The Mercury*,

The Advertiser and *The Daily Telegraph* appealed for more donations, saying that 'the quest to raise $500,000 has not met with the spontaneous response expected'.

A month before the Ludgrove's auction another Bradman cap, surprisingly a second 1946-47 cap marked 'D.G. Bradman', was auctioned by Christie's in Britain. As the Tim Biles 1946-47 cap had been sold in 1995, also by Christie's, how was there another cap? *The Age*[4] interviewed Rick Pike, Christie's marketing consultant. He was 'quite satisfied' that the cap was the one originally presented to Bradman and worn by him for most of the series. It was a small cap, which matched Bradman's size.

Pike said the Tim Biles cap was a second or a replacement. 'Somewhere along the line, Bradman has used a spare. There were many documented cases of Australian international players using spare caps during series in the 40s,' he said.

Further clouding the issue were reports in *The Sydney Morning Herald* that Keith Miller and Bradman swapped caps before the first Test of 1946-47 and kept them all summer. Quoting Miller from Britain's *Daily Mail*: 'You know how fastidious the Don was. That morning in Brisbane he fiddled around with the cap that he'd been given and complained it didn't fit, so I tossed him mine and said, "Try that." It fitted perfectly. He wore it throughout the series.' Miller believed that the two caps had the initials DGB and KRM written inside them and had no idea where his cap, with DGB, went.

Christie's were adamant that the cap was Bradman's[5] and said it had been handed to Ron Saggers, the Australian wicketkeeper, and then passed on to the present vendor. The controversy seems not to have deterred the eventual owner, an Australian living in London, who paid £35,250 ($88,835) for it.

Given that amount, the expectations during Ludgrove's 1948 cap campaign that it would sell for about $500,000 seemed ludicrously extravagant, even allowing for a premium for the association with the famous 1948 Invincibles tour.

On 7 July, 2003 the ABC's *Media Watch* reported[6] that one of its representatives had asked the National Australia Bank about the campaign account balance. It was reported to be between $8000 and $9000. Obviously the appeal would not be buying the cap. Another buyer was required.

Unexpectedly on the 30 June, 2003, only days after the 1946-47 Bradman cap achieved a public auction record of $88,000 in Britain, Ludgrove's announced that an unnamed NSW collector had paid $425,000 for the Invincibles cap. In the *Herald Sun* that day Halbish, the chairman of Ludgrove's, said: 'It is higher than the world record price of Sir Donald's 1947-48 Indian series baggy green that Ludgrove's sold before auction in February for an undisclosed sum. At that time, a Bradman sculpture that sold for $180,000 was the yardstick.'

Halbish added: 'News Ltd's campaign showed that the people of Australia wanted the cap. They responded with spirit, but the private offer was too significant for the owner to refuse an immediate sale.'

In the reports carried by the *Herald Sun*, *ABC Online* and *The Sydney Morning Herald* of 30 June, the buyer was unnamed but identified as a former winner of *Who Wants to be a Millionaire?* 'The new owner is planning to put the cap on public display,' Halbish said.[7]

Given his exploits on national TV, the buyer was soon identified as Tim Serisier,[8] who had just won $250,000 on the popular quiz show. 'The Invincible cap belongs on public display and not in a bank vault,' he was quoted as saying. The cap did go on display; firstly at some regional shopping centres.[9] It was then part of a roadshow presented by Cricket Australia and Travelex (a Cricket Australia sponsor) which visited capital cities and regional centres in early 2004.[10] A photograph of the cap sitting in a perspex box was featured in Cricket Australia's *Insight* newsletter.[11]

News Ltd subsequently offered refunds for donations made to the fruitless endeavour, yet they still claimed that the campaign had been a success as Serisier had learned about the cap through the newspapers' appeal.

In another interesting twist, John Howard, Australia's most public cricket tragic, and his new Goods and Services Tax (GST) came into play. According to a report on Pakistan's *Dawn.com* on 10 September, 2003, before leaving to collect the cap in Britain Serisier asked the Australian Tax Office and Australian Customs if the cap would attract the 10 per cent GST. The Tax Office responded that it probably would but Customs told him that a cap is a cap, which he took to mean the baggy green would be regarded as a piece of clothing and be exempt from the tax. Upon his return, he was advised that he was liable for GST; he paid it the day after his return. 'It's disappointing because it will discourage Australian investors from bringing heritage items into this country,' Serisier said.

Based on the reported price of $425,000 the tax added $42,500. The cap had cost almost the half a million dollars predicted.[12] According to *The Sydney Morning Herald*,[13] the GST liability was due to the cap being a collectable item, which customs had advised. This was 'a view backed up by the Prime Minister, John Howard, an avid cricket fan'.

Rumour dogged Ludgroves, especially when stories of auction irregularities relating to a bat signed by W.G. Grace and Bradman aired on the Nine network's *A Current Affair*. The former federal minister John Brown had consigned the bat to Ludgroves aiming to raise money for a charity. The bat was knocked down at auction way below the reserve, and neither the new owner nor Ludgroves were prepared to recompense Brown or the charity for the amount he believed it was worth. It was revealed that Michael Ludgrove had resigned as a director of the business and in 2004 an administrator was appointed. Creditors subsequently accepted 30 cents in the dollar.

Six months after the auction the *Herald Sun's* 'Spy' reported that a London source close to the British vendor said that the sale figure for the 1948 cap may have been $360,000. Subsequent investigation has led me to believe that an intermediary 'bought' the cap from Ludgrove's for the lower figure, which was the amount used to pay out the vendor, then the cap was sold for the $425,000 pre-auction.

Whatever the case, speculation was rife. Was the cap worth $425,000 (plus GST)? Would it have achieved a similar price in a public auction? Would subsequent pieces emulate this record? With huge figures being bandied about, more caps and more mystery were in store.

Much of the controversy is due to the fact that the cap's history has not been adequately researched and documented. Auction houses and collections have tried to establish the cap's ownership and year of issue without having all sales records and all the caps in collections available to them.

★★★★★

A year later, another baggy green, this time reported to be Bradman's cap from his record-breaking first tour to Britain in 1930 went to auction at Christie's. This cap, undated and made by Harding's Mercery, was given by Bradman to Leonard Mills, a steward on an Orient liner. The Australians travelled to and from England on the Nairana and the catalogue states that the cap was undated. (This is unusual. Pre-1930 caps bore no date, but a Clarrie Grimmett cap sold in 1998 was clearly dated 1930.)

Christie's claimed that Grimmett's cap, which was auctioned in May 1998 was 'specially manufactured' for him, with the inference that the date had been added especially for Grimmett and that it did not appear on other 1930 caps. The 'specially manufactured' mark on the label was printed on all 1930 caps but in this situation it was taken to have a far more specific meaning.

The press has never questioned the lack of date on the so-called Bradman cap, mainly because there has been no reference book produced that has collated information from museums, auction houses and official sources on the changes to baggy greens over the years. From 1928-29 to 1932-33 the cap underwent several changes in design, the inclusion of the date being the major one.

Irrespective of the possible misdating of the cap, it was offered and sold as Bradman's 1930 baggy. The then 20-year-old performed brilliantly on that tour. The cap was sold for £35,850 ($93,790). Although this was less than the prices achieved pre-auction by Ludgroves for the other caps – $200,000 and almost $500,000 – it was still a significant amount. It remains the highest price achieved for a baggy green at a public auction.

★★★★★

Two other 1930 caps have been offered at auction: Ted a'Beckett's cap was offered at Charles Leski's in Melbourne on 13 December, 2001 and Tim Wall's at Leski's on 28 June, 2006. Both bore the date 1930. The Grimmett and Wall caps bore the manufacturer's name, Scholium, an English cap maker.

To further explain the lack of date on this 1930 Bradman cap, Christie's cited the donation of Bradman's 1928-29 cap to the State Library of South Australia. Bradman had given the cap to a neighbour, Peter Dunham (a schoolboy) in the 1950s. Christie's reasoned that if this cap, made by Harding's Mercery, was Bradman's then the cap made by Harding's going to auction, also undated and given by Bradman after 1930, must be from that tour. Bradman had played only two series up to that point. After 1930 caps were made by Farmer's of Sydney.

It is possible caps were made by two manufacturers for the same tour. David Studham from the Melbourne Cricket Club's library suggested this in late 2006. The date does not appear on Bradman's cap in any of the images from that tour that I have seen. The only photograph showing a dated cap is a studio shot with Bradman in cap and blazer. Possibly the players used a new cap from Hardings on tour – or Bradman did – and the 1930 dated caps came later. Either that or Bradman chose to wear an earlier model.

With the market so buoyant it seemed inevitable that the 1946-47 cap given to Tim Biles and now owned by Cam Tingley would come on the market. In September, 2004, Michael Ludgrove, by then at Lawson's Menzies, tried to sell it, with estimates of $300,000 to $500,000. While there were five pages of description, there was no mention of the cap's manufacturer, the label or any owner's name. The cap was passed in.

A year later the same auction house presented the cap again and it was sold for a reported $95,400.

★★★★★

In November 2004 the final Bradman cap to appear came on the market. Sensationally, it was another 1948. Imagine how Tim Serisier felt. When he bought his 1948 cap in July 2003, there was just one Invincibles cap and only six Bradman caps in existence. Eighteen months later there were nine caps and, most dramatically, two from his famous farewell series.

This final cap from 1948 was offered to the State Library of South Australia by Kevin Truscott. Bradman had given it to Kevin's father after the 1948 tour and it had remained within the family. The late Barry Gibbs, the then manager of the Bradman Collection, researched the circumstances of the dual caps and uncovered the existence of contracts specifying that the players were issued with two caps. Now on display in the library and its website, the cap, made by Farmer's, is marked in handwriting 'DG Bradman'.

The front page of Adelaide's *The Advertiser*, adorned with

a colour photograph, proudly proclaimed: 'A gift to us. The Don's cap comes home'.[14]

Given the vast sums achieved for Bradman caps and the bizarre twists and turns surrounding their marketing, Kevin Truscott's donation was very generous. And it was fitting that the 1948 cap came home this way, as a donation, given that Sir Donald had given away his caps as gifts.

Other Bradman caps which are on public display at the Bradman Museum were originally donated. A NSW cap given by Bradman to the vendor was bought in 2002 for an undisclosed sum. A South Australian cap was given directly to the museum.

MF

References

1 Introduced by the Howard government on 1 July, 2000 as a 10 per cent impost on virtually all service and trade transactions within Australia.
2 'Bradman a Tribute' – *Inside Edge*, 2001.
3 *The Daily Telegraph* (Sydney), 21/5/2003.
4 *The Age*, 24/6/2003.
5 *AM*, ABC Radio 25/6/2003, Andrew McVinish, Christie's cricket expert.
6 *Media Watch*, 7/1/2003. www.abc.net.au/mediawatch/transcipts/s896810.htm.
7 *Herald Sun*, 30/6/2003 - Rod Nicholson.
8 *The Border Mail*, 1/7/2003.
9 Coffs Harbour City Council media release, 2/10/2003.
10 Travelex press release. 9/1/2004..
11 *Insight*, February-April 2003.
12 *Dawn.com* – the website of Pakistan's most widely circulated English language newspaper.
13 *SMH*, 9/9/2003.
14 *The Advertiser*, 25/11/2004.

— CAP IN HAND —

Terry James Jenner and Kerry James O'Keeffe share more than a second given name and an intimate understanding of the science of leg-spin bowling.

These proud, wily craftsmen, who debuted two months apart against England in 1970-71, lost their way in mid-life and needed the help of the game and its finest people to rediscover their pride and dignity and return to the public consciousness.

O'Keeffe, who has brought his own language to the broadcasting of the game on ABC radio, describes this period of his life as being as being 'in the driest of gullies'. Throughout the 1990s he worked at a string of temporary, unsuitable and modestly paid jobs and felt as dispirited as he was unfulfilled.

Jenner, too, knows how dry and empty the gully can be. Renowned as coach and advisor to the peerless Shane Warne, 'TJ', as he is universally known, spent 18 months in prison at the close of the 1980s after embezzling money from an employer to pay gambling debts.

Historically Australia has been wonderfully served by leg-spinners, and Don Bradman and his fellow selectors believed it would be these fabled slow men who could bolster Australia's sagging stocks against England in 1970-71 and particularly in the West Indies in 1973.

Of the five Tests Jenner and O'Keeffe played together, four were in the Caribbean. And as was the case against England in 1970-71 when Johnny Gleeson was still mystifying opponents generally and Geoff Boycott in particular, Jenner, O'Keeffe, Keith Stackpole and Ian Chappell also were gainfully employed with their leg breaks at various times. And in the Caribbean John Watkins, a remarkable selection, was in the wings.

Jenner received his first baggy green cap for the opening Test with England at the Gabba in November 1970 and O'Keeffe his for the fifth Test of the series.

The only time they played together against England was in the dramatic final Test, Ian Chappell's first as captain, which is remembered as much for the crowd disturbances and England walk-off that followed the felling of Jenner by a John Snow bouncer as for England's 62-run victory to regain the Ashes.

These days whenever he examines his first baggy green Jenner gives thanks that he had presented it to his father, Arthur, soon after he played his final Test against the West Indies in November 1975. In his heart he knows that had it been in his possession when the darkest days descended he would have sold it.

'I'm glad my father had it when I was really doing it hard. There is no doubt I would have sold it and for very little too,' said Jenner.

Before his death at the age of 84 in 2002, Arthur returned the cap to Jenner who has bequeathed it to his daughter Trudianne along with an Australian sweater and a mini bat bearing the signatures of a host of international luminaries who celebrated the centenary of Test cricket being played at Adelaide Oval in 1984.

O'Keeffe's first baggy green was still in his possession when he reached his 'driest of gullies' and he is still haunted by the memory of selling it for $5000 to a collector in country NSW.

'The dearest thing I had had to go to get me through a tough time,' said O'Keeffe with considerable emotion. 'It really hurt and nagged me that while I had not cheapened it I had seen a dollar value whereas I had never seen a dollar value on the cap. Not ever.

'Even though the players are wealthy now they still revere the cap and I had that reverence for it. But my situation affected my regard for it. I regretted it at the time but now must accept it and be thankful I still have a cap.'

That a baggy green has its own shelf in a walk-in robe at his home is the result of an act of great selflessness by the sons of one of O'Keeffe's cricketing pals, the late John McLaughlin.

In the mid-1970s when O'Keeffe despaired of regaining a place in the Australian team he was grateful for the constant support and reassurance of his friend. And it proved well founded when O'Keeffe was selected for the first Test with Pakistan at Adelaide in December 1976, almost three years since his previous appearance, against New Zealand in Auckland.

O'Keeffe concedes that he was tired and emotional at a Christmas function when he spontaneously presented McLaughlin with a baggy green.

Since the death of their father, Peter and Mark McLaughlin had heard O'Keeffe during cricket broadcasts lamenting the fact he did not have a cherished baggy green cap.

Late in 2006 the boys contacted O'Keeffe and suggested he meet them at the Kyle Bay Bowling Club where he used to drink and chew the cud with their father. To O'Keeffe's unbridled joy the brothers produced from a brown paper bag a baggy green cap with the initials KO'K clearly visible on the tag. Such had been the Christmas celebrations all those summers before that O'Keeffe had forgotten he had parted with his precious cap.

The boys knew what their father would have expected of them and they honoured his memory with a gesture that effectively completed O'Keeffe's rehabilitation to a normal life as Australia's 253rd Test cricketer.

MC

8

VARIATIONS AND ODDITIES

O VER the years, there have been numerous cricket caps produced for official and unofficial Australian representative teams. The production of these caps can be seen as a homage to the Test cap. Once the 1899 cap established the appropriate colour and emblem, most other representative caps have been of a similar green with the variations on the badge based on the common theme of the kangaroo and the emu.

In 1913 a team organised by Edgar Mayne toured North America. This was an Australian representative XI but with no official patronage. The badge on the cap and blazer contained a kangaroo and emu in gold wire either side of a large 'A'.

The 1919 AIF team cap that belonged to Bert Oldfield resides at Lord's. Made in England by George Lewin & Co, it is dark blue and has a rising sun badge (based on the Australian Army insignia) as well as a crown with a scroll. The inscription is 'Australian Commonwealth Military Forces'. Oldfield's is one of three known; another is at the MCC Museum in Melbourne and the third with a private collector.

Arthur Mailey organised a private but officially sanctioned tour of Canada and the US in 1932. A cap and blazer were produced incorporating the kangaroo, emu and rising sun. These surrounded a large 'A' with 'Canadian American Tour 1932' in the scroll. A blazer pocket was auctioned at

A proud veteran … Herbie Collins, a successful Australian captain of the 1920s, in his AIF cap.   **Photo: Ronald Cardwell**

Ludgrove's and a cap is now on display at the MCC Museum. On this tour the capped players wore their Australian caps while those who were not Australian players wore the tour cap. This appears to have been based on the 1912 cap.

An umpire's blazer which belonged to Bodyline official George Hele contained the cricket coat of arms but the two panels which normally have a white background are yellow.[1] It seems that was the only time the colours of the coat of arms were varied, a reasonable decision to differentiate between a player's attire and an umpire's.

The Australian War Memorial in Canberra has a photograph of a cricket team in a prisoner of war camp in Germany in 1943 with the players wearing homemade baggy green caps. This is a poignant reminder that the cap is a unifying national symbol.[2]

The July 2003 Ludgrove's catalogue contained the image of an unusual baggy green. Lot # 318 was from the Keith Johnson collection. It was described as a 'Baggy Green Test cap, green wool, coat of arms worked in gold wire and coloured thread with early motto "Advance Australia"; Foster of London maker's label, possibly commissioned by Keith Johnson for the 1945 services match.' This would appear to be incorrect as a services blazer which was auctioned by Mullock Madeley in 2001[3] contained the Australian coat of arms (and states' badges) with 'Victory Tests, England India, 1945' embroidered below.

Brenton Siggs, who produced a signed bat commemorating the Victory Test, met many of the players and never saw a cap. He was unsure if one was produced and suggested that maybe each wore their particular service headgear; for instance Keith Miller's RAAF XI cap which is now on display at the Australian War Memorial.

The 1960 Australian 2nd XI blazer featured three stumps in white with bats either side and a red ball on top. The word 'Australia' was in the scroll with 1960 below it.[4]

In 1967 an Australian representative team visited New Zealand for a 10-match tour. They played four matches against New Zealand, which were not accredited as Test matches. The cap was a traditional baggy green, embroidered with 'NZ Tour 1967'. This was the first time the series opponents were listed on a cap rather than just the date of the series.

Various Australian 'rebel' tours have used a cap. Possibly in deference to the baggy green, for legal reasons or to establish a separate identity, these were yellow rather than green. The caps for Kerry Packer's World Series Cricket were yellow (sometimes described as wattle gold) with the WSC logo – the three stumps and ball. They also follow a slimmer, more English style. This was again a counterpoint to the establishment Australian cap. For the inaugural 1977-78 season, the badge was directly embroidered but from the following summer it was sewn on.

The caps for the rebel tours to South Africa in 1985-86 and 1986-87 were also predominately gold. Best described as a golf hat, it had panels of different material and contained the logo of a kangaroo and a springbok on a red cricket ball.

*****

Initially seen as a threat to traditional cricket, the helmet is here to stay. The use of a helmet is now compulsory for every child batting in organised cricket in NSW. Players rarely, if at all, bat in a cap during a Test match so the helmet is almost the extension of the cap, a 21st century baggy green. There is further evidence to support this.

When Cricket Australia registered its brands in 2002-03 the new logo was included on all marketing paraphernalia, reports, websites and the players' apparel. The new logo now adorns the Test and ODI shirts, fielding hats and ODI caps. Like the Test cap, the green Test helmet retained the cricket coat of arms. Further strengthening this re-evaluation of the Test helmet is the fact that the yellow ODI variation was phased out in 2002. Now players wear the green helmet in both forms of the game.

Michael Slater, famous for kissing his helmet when he scored a century on his first appearance in a Test at Lord's, explained the differing affections for cap and helmet, and encapsulated the possible inclusion of the helmet as a modern equivalent to the cap. 'I suppose it would have been a better feeling to have kissed the cap at Lord's but I kissed the badge and it's the same on both.'[5]

The helmet is a work in progress. With the introduction of protective gear it was initially a motorcycle helmet, but much tinkering has occurred over the years to improve the helmet's comfort and durability. The early helmets were heavy, hot and made communication difficult. Albion continued researching and produced a more comfortable variation in 2003. This was the lighter one-piece, injection-moulded, plastic model first used by Michael Bevan. This helmet lost the embroidered badge and had a pad print of the coat of arms. Acceptance of this helmet was slow as the players complained

Under a lid ... Mark Taylor in England in 1997. Modern batsmen rarely take strike without wearing a helmet. **Photo: Varley Picture Agency**

that they had not been consulted in the design process. This harks back to the players' long-held sense of ownership of the cap, the badge and its design. At the time of writing a new generation of helmet, a combination of technology and heritage, was soon to be released. The coat of arms was to feature prominently on it.

With insurance and occupational health and safety issues so prevalent, helmet wear will increase. With skin cancer concerns also growing, wide-brim sunhats might also become compulsory. Many cricket clubs now issue these sunhats as official kit to the children's teams rather than traditional cricket caps. In a few years, it is possible that the cap will be seen as anachronistic, similar to belts and buckles from 19th century cricket.

This would not be the case if more players carried as deep a sense of the cap's history as Justin Langer. Batting against the Indians in Sydney in January 2000, Langer put aside his helmet and called for his 1900 replica cap when he was nearing his century. He kissed the badge and went on to score 223 although he had his 'tin hat' on when he passed the 200 mark.

Similarly Steve Waugh, who rarely batted in his cap, had it on against Pakistan in Sharjah in 2002. On a placid pitch against a dual spin attack he had the opportunity to achieve a rare feat. With last partner Glenn McGrath watching from the other end, Waugh advanced from 83 to 103 in an over. 'Scoring a hundred with a six and the baggy green on top of your head – it doesn't come much better than that,' he said.[6]

Will collectors unable to afford the increasingly expensive caps turn their attention to the only other piece of headwear carrying the relic from a different era – the helmet with the cricket coat of arms? Or will they begin to collect the various ODI caps, the first of which was a baggy yellow of the same design as its famous gum-tree green counterpart. Or will they collect the baggy greens worn by Australia's highly successful women cricketers, who are now officially full members of the Australian cricket system.

*****

There have been a few recent additions to the saga of the now highly valued baggy green.

The celebrated repair of Steve Waugh's battered old cap resulted in a peak-shaped piece being removed. What to do with a piece of one of Australia's most celebrated caps?

The Steve Waugh Foundation, an organisation that assists those who fail to receive funding from other charities, was planning to offer 11 positions as foundation patrons. These would all be members of the Steve Waugh Foundation First XI. It was decided to reward those patrons, each of whom was contributing $250,000, with something symbolic of Waugh's career and commitment to the cause.

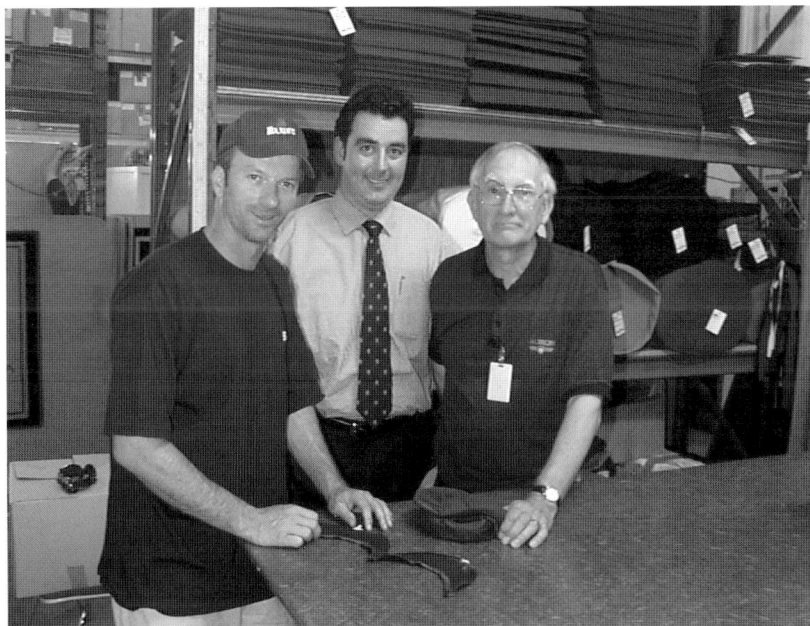

In for a makeover ... Steve Waugh was on hand at Albion C&D when his beloved baggy green cap was repaired. With Waugh are Albion's Ross Barrat and Clemente Izurieta. **Photo: Albion C&D**

A piece of the cap's old cloth was mounted on the blades of 11 bats that he had used in a first-class match. Each bat was then framed with photographic tributes and a handwritten message of gratitude from Waugh. The result is an interesting sidelight to the baggy green story.

After Albion C&D repaired and cleaned Steve Waugh's cap, national sales manager Ross Barrat realised that the years of beer and sweat were taking a toll on the fabric. And with more players wearing the one cap for 100 or more Tests the baggy greens were being loved to death. Subsequent steam clean jobs for the caps of Adam Gilchrist and Justin Langer confirmed Barrat's fears.

Barrat thought of a way to protect the caps from dirty gear, boots and spills. The result, now given as a gift from the company to each player, is a bag made from green cotton embroidered with the cricket coat of arms, the player's name and his Test number. Steve Waugh was given the first bag, followed by Gilchrist and Langer. It was first presented only to those whose caps needed attention, but is now being done for all players, many of whom hang the cap bags on their locker door in the Australian dressing room. Other countries who buy their caps from Albion have adopted this practice.

In 2000 160 Test players gathered in Sydney for an inaugural reunion – one open to every former Australian Test cricketer. This event was inspired by Allan Border and Greg Matthews. The evening also included the naming of the Team of the Century.

With Test numbers being introduced on players' shirts for the 2001-02 series the reunion presented an opportunity to present all past players with a record of their chronological Test number. In July 2003 CA and the Australian Cricketers' Association (ACA) held a dinner in Sydney and 147 of the 197 living Test players attended. Another 15 'attended' via video link from London.

Albion made a two thirds-sized miniature cap which was presented to each player. The cap contained a scaled-down embroidered coat of arms. The ACB had each cap boxed with a glass top and an engraved plaque. Interestingly a number of former players have asked Albion to embroider their Test number onto the back of their miniature caps.

The traditions and legacy of the baggy green continue to evolve, and the richness of its history deepens.

MF

References

1 Christie's Australia Cricket Auction, 27/6/1999. # 454. Estimate $4000-$6000. Passed in.
2 www.awm.gov/stolenyears/ww2/germany/story3.html. In Hohenfels, P02071.029.
3 Auction, 8/12/2001. Item # 275. Worn by Cec Pepper. With a reserve of £350-500, it sold for £330.
4 Offered in a Boxshalls # 4 sale, 12/5/2000, Item # 171.
5 *The Baggy Green* – Viv Jenkins, New Holland Publishers, 1998.
6 AAP sports news, 21/10/2002.

Appendix
THE BAGGY GREEN AT THE NEW MCG

THE development of the Australian Test cricket colours tells a multitude of stories and reveals so much about our history. Accordingly, the caps, blazers and other items of apparel are desirable acquisitions for collecting institutions such as the Melbourne Cricket Club Museum and the National Sports Museum.

These objects, whether they are for museum display, interpretation or research, help to articulate the story of a player, a match or even an entire tour. Each story, social or sporting, can add to our understanding of the traditions and status of, for example, the baggy green cap in Australian society.

The very broad responsibilities of the MCC's museums department reflect the club's commitment to its sports-related heritage activities, which is prominent in its mission statement and values. The club is also committed to the International Council of Museums' (ICOM) code of ethics, as well as the Museums Australia code of ethics and the museum accreditation program standards.

The adoption of these standards is one of the key differences between museums and private collectors. While the private collector rarely formally studies the cultural significance of the items he has acquired, this is one of the main activities museums pursue on behalf of the public.

Obtaining objects for the collections held or managed by the MCC is driven by the desire to add cultural capital rather than financial capital. A range of issues informs the decisions about material being considered for acquisition.

Museums such as the MCG's do not strive to acquire every baggy green cap. The decision to acquire a cap rests on whether it is relevant to holdings, whether it fits into the collections policy, and whether the collecting institution is able to house it, care for it and make it accessible to a wider audience. So, while a particular baggy green may be seen by a collector as a 'must', a collecting institution will probably be working to more specific guidelines.

Once identified as having merit and relevance, an object may be secured on three different bases – donation, loan or purchase. Donation is the preferred means as this ensures transfer of ownership to the institution and often affords the acquiring body a higher level of flexibility in the long-term access, display and interpretation of the object.

Additionally, donations may be made through the federal government's Cultural Gifts Program whereby, following independent evaluation and review, donors are able to gain a tax offset against the agreed value of the donated material.

One of the key differences between a museum and the private collector is the mandate to undertake an educational role for the wider community. Under the ICOM code of ethics, a museum is bound to 'provide opportunities for the appreciation, understanding and promotion of the natural and cultural heritage'. A prime means of doing this is the display and interpretation of collections.

Research, display and interpretation within the MCG have been a commitment of the club since its library was established in 1873. Earlier displays of Australian Test caps were mounted in several locations in the Members' Pavilion, the Australian Gallery of Sport and Olympic Museum (AGOS-OM) and the Australian Cricket Hall of Fame (ACHOF).

Display and interpretation facilities were significantly increased in area and quality as part of the redevelopment of the Northern Stand at the MCG. Material is displayed on a range of levels from the informal short term to the formal and structured museum spaces. This entails 'heritage dressing' of public spaces (such as dining rooms and bars) and the interpretative, themed displays within the pavilion (such as the military forces case and seasonally rotating display cases).

Formal exhibition spaces in the new grandstand comprise the MCC Museum and the National Sports Museum. The MCC Museum opened to wide acclaim on November 15, 2006, and the National Sports Museum opened on March 12, 2008. These two spaces occupy almost 2200 square metres and display more than 4000 objects linked to Australian sporting life and culture.

While many people only see the display and interpretation component of museums and galleries, this is only one

Pride of place ... Don Bradman shows the way at the new Baggy Green Room at the National Sports Museum at the MCG. **Photo: John Gollings**

aspect of the collection. Placement of the objects in a social and historical context can be one of the key results of research.

For example, the tradition of players wearing team colours and being 'capped' goes back to the early development of organised competitive sport, where participants wore caps to distinguish the colours of their house, school or team. Over the years the cricket cap has become the unmistakable symbol of a team. The presentation of a representative cap for national and regional teams has become a tradition in a number of team sports.

Not everybody would know that the baggy green cap has not been worn by all Australian Test cricketers. The early pioneers played under different colours, logos or arms. Nor would everybody know that Australian cricket teams are the only national teams that do not play under the official national coat of arms. This makes the MCC's early caps, blazers and other symbols of the team's colours such evocative and useful tools in telling the story of the development of Australia's international cricketing history.

Being able to place similar or contrasting objects together can enable staff to explain such topics as manufacture, style, use or significance. Then there is the impact of being able to mount a mass display of like objects. The Baggy Green Room in the NSM is a prime example of this strategy.

Of interest here is the comparison of a range of caps held by the MCC and the Bradman Collection at the State Library of South Australia that led to the clarification of provenance of a significant cap from the late 1920s.

A cap had been offered to the library but, as it had the words 'Advance Australia' and no date, the library staff wanted to date it and corroborate this with examples from the same period. They knew it was pre-1930, but wanted to compare it to another 1928-29 series cap, which the MCC had. Consultation with the MCC librarian and comparisons with ones from this era in the MCC collection revealed that this Bradman cap was from his first international season, 1928-29.

As a result of such strong holdings of baggy green caps, NSM exhibition designers decided that their appeal demanded iconic status within the cricket exhibition.

With more than 20 baggy greens on display from famous players such as Don Bradman, Keith Miller, Neil Harvey and Richie Benaud, the Baggy Green Room underlines the unique nature of this part of our Test cricketers' uniform. Seeing a wide range of caps in the one location has not hitherto been practicable within the MCG, but this display enables the visitor to examine at close hand the evolution of the cap's style and ornamentation. It also shows the value of sustained and focused collecting through the MCC Museum and Australian Gallery of Sport and Olympic Museum over more than 40 years.

In the National Sports Museum cricket occupies one of the seven principal exhibition spaces that celebrate more than 50 sports. This component of the NSM, titled 'Backyard to Baggy Green', offers Cricket Australia the opportunity to display a wide range of key perpetual trophies in their care. The title is taken from the Cricket Australia Strategic Plan and provides a logical framework for a journey through the space, the journey of Australian cricket from backyard to the Test arena. Visitors will be shown a wealth of historical and contemporary photographs, artefacts and images through a range of multimedia installations.

The Baggy Green Room will be located deep in the heart of the NSM. The centrepiece is a life-size bronze sculpture by Mitch Mitchell of Don Bradman which has a backdrop of showcases featuring more than 20 baggy greens. While obviously a tribute to an outstanding sportsman, it is also a larger tribute to all those who have worn the Test cap. The display is placed in the context of the iconic individual status of Bradman, of cricket as a sport for all and of the history of the game.

When focusing on the baggy greens as individual objects it quickly becomes apparent that there is a wide range of associations through the fame of the individuals who wore them. Establishing which player owned or wore which cap is critical to the management and interpretation of each object.

Such is the strength of this iconic piece that the design of the space relies on the attraction of the individual object and therefore has minimal interpretative text. Discussion, research and interpretation on subjects strongly linked to the baggy green cap, such as the cap as a symbol of national tradition, national pride, representation and aspiration, are outside the scope of this article but provide rich material for future NSM projects.

David Studham and Richard Ferguson
Melbourne Cricket Club

Baggy Green Sales – by sale year

Figures excluding Bradman Cap sales

Year	Number	$ Value	$ Ave	Number	$ Value	$ Ave	Year	Notes
1988	2	1,720	860	2	1,720	860	1988	1997 Incld Trumper
1995	1	7,500	7,500	0	–	–	1995	Cap at $28,750 if
1997	4	39,652	9,913	4	39,652	9,913	1997	excl. ave $3,634
1998	7	23,567	3,367	7	23,567	3,367	1998	1998 ex $45 matthews
1999	12	105,958	8,830	12	105,958	8,830	1999	
2000	12	97,102	8,092	12	97,102	8,092	2000	
2001	12	138,628	11,552	12	138,628	11,552	2001	
2002	15	137,431	9,162	15	137,431	9,162	2002	
2003	18	798,799	44,378	15	104,964	6,998	2003	
2004	5	200,435	40,087	4	105,050	26,263	2004	
2005	16	243,586	15,224	16	243,586	15,224	2005	
2006	13	214,990	16,538	13	214,990	16,538	2006	
2007	4	34,669	8,667	4	34,669	8,667	2007	
Total	121	2,044,037	16,893	116	1,247,317	10,753		
Matthews	1	45,000		+Bradman	796,720			
Grand Total	122	2,089,037		+Matthews	45,000			
					2,089,037			

Excluding 5 Bradman Caps Sold & Matthews cap

Period	# caps	Total Sales	Ave price
1988-2003	79	649,022	8,215
2004-2007	37	598,295	16,170
	116	$1,247,317	$10,753

Figures are from auctions held before 28 June, 2007

Baggy Green Sales – by the Caps Decade

Figures excluding Bradman Cap sales

Year	Number	$ Total	$ Ave	Number	$ Total ex Br	$ Ave	YEAR
1890	1	28,750	28,750	1	28,750	28,750	1890
1900	1	83,000	83,000	1	83,000	83,000	1900
1910	0	-	-	0	-	-	1910
1920	3	14,390	14,390	3	14,390	4,797	1920
1930	13	229,949	17,688	12	134,564	11,214	1930
1940	11	835,350	75,941	7	134,015	19,145	1940
1950	26	338,999	13,038	26	338,999	13,038	1950
1960	29	250,833	8,649	29	250,833	8,649	1960
1970	3	42,032	14,011	3	42,032	14,011	1970
1980	2	15,015	7,508	2	15,015	7,508	1980
1990	2	18,517	9,259	2	18,517	9,259	1990
1970-Today	29	172,202	5,938	29	172,202	5,938	1970-Day
2000	1	15,000	15,000	1	15,000	15,000	2000
Total	121	2,044,037	16,893	116	1,247,317	10,753	
Matthews	1	45,000	Matthews	1	45,000		Matthews
				5	796,720		Bradman
Grand Total	122	2,089,037		122	2,089,037		

Average Values by Period

Period	# caps	Total sales	Ave price
1899<1950	24	394,719	16,447
1950<1970	58	589,832	10,170
Post 1970	33	247,766	7,508
2000 Millenium	1	15,000	15,000

Note: Since 1972 caps have been undated. Where the exact date of a modern cap is not known the figures are included in the 1970-Today period. Some caps without dates have however been sold by players and the date of wear actually specified. These have been included in the figures for the 1980s or 1990s.

Brothers in arms ... Damien Fleming, Justin Langer and Jason Gillespie observe a minute's silence for Sir Donald Bradman who had died two days earlier. First Test, Mumbai, February 2001. **Photo: Mark Ray**

Index

memorabilia, 4, 18, 68–75
  baseball 87
  values 82–9, 124–5
Mendis, Duleep 30
Merriman, Bob 8
Miandad, Javed 30
Miller, Colin 9
Miller, Keith 30, 48, 76, 83, 84, 85, 99, 111, 122
Mills, Leonard 102
miner's pick 39, 52
Misson, Frank 17, 66–7, 76
Moody, Tom 13
Morris, Arthur 16, 27, 28, 29, 83, **97**
Mortlock Collection 72
Moss, Jeff 81
Muller, Scott 9
Mullock Madeley Auctions 83, 111
multiple caps 56–7, 79–80, 96–7, 99, 103–4
Mumbai 28, 80, 126
Murdoch, Billy 34
museums, continuing work of 118–23

national selectors, appointment 37
National Sports Museum (NSM) 70, 71, 118, 121–3
  Baggy Green Room 71, **120**, 121–2
Nawaz, Sarfraz 81
Nazar, Mudassar 81
New Zealand 13, 27, 30, 76, 80, 91, 107, 111
News Ltd 95, 98, 100, 101
O'Brien, Leo 70
O'Keeffe, Kerry 106–8
Old Trafford 18
Oldfield, Bert 83, 109
one-day cricket 12, 60, 84, 112, 114
one test players 79–81
O'Neill, Gwen 76–7, **78**
O'Neill, Norm 76–7, **78**
O'Reilly, Bill 25–6
Oval, The 34, 61, 91

Pakistan 9, 14, 30, 65, 76, 81, 107, 114
Pascoe, Len 25–6
Patel, Jasu 76
Pelegrini, Carlo 35
Phillips (London) 82, 84
Pike, Rick 99
Ponsford, Bill 6
Ponting, Ricky xi, 9, 14–15, **45**, 90, 98

Potts and Wilkinson 47
presentation ceremonies 8–10, 43–4, 46, 57
prisoners of war (Germany) 111
psychological edge xi, 11, 62–3
Pullen, Reg 28

Ransford, Vernon 54
Raper, Johnny 30
Ratnayeke, Ravi 30
rebel tours 111–12
Redpath, Ian 27, 77–8, 79, 80
Reece, Barry 'Nugget' 76–7
Reece, Ray 76–7
repairs 116–17
Richards, Viv 30, 66
Richardson, Vic 19
Rigg, Keith 70
rituals 15–16, 61
Rixon, Steve 28
Robert, Andy 30
Robins, Richard 90–1, 98
Robins, Walter 91
Rogers, Chris 57, 79
Rowan Glasgow 47, 72

Sabina Park, Kingston 29
Saggers, Ron 99
Sawle, Lawrie 14
Scholium 47, 51, 103
schoolchildren 65–6
Sellers, Rex 80
Serisier, Tim 100, 101, 104
Sharpham, Peter 40
Sheahan, Paul 79
sheep 39, 52
Sheridan, Percy 37
ship 39, 52
shirts
  named 32
  numbered 13
Siggs, Brenton 111
Simpson, Bob 16, 17, 23, 24, 30, 80
skull cap 40, 42, 43, 49, 58, 72
Slater, Keith 59
Slater, Michael 9, 112
Snow, John 106
Sobers, Sir Garfield 87
South Africa 13, 15, 18, 30, 52, 55, 65, 73, 79, 80, 92
Southern Cross 35, 37, 39, 52, 60
Spofforth, Fred 33, 34

The oldest known Australian Test cap … this cap is owned by English cricket historian Keith Hayhurst and is on display at the Old Trafford ground in Manchester. Hayhurst was given the cap by descendants of Richard Barlow, a famous all-rounder for Lancashire and England. In the tourists' match against the North of England at Trent Bridge in September 1884, Barlow took 10 wickets and made a century against an attack that included Fred Spofforth. The story goes that Australian captain Billy Murdoch was so impressed by Barlow's performance that he came onto the field at the end of the match and gave the Englishman his Australian cap, saying: "Barlow, I take my cap off to you." Research suggests that the cap is actually from Australia's previous tour to England in 1882 when the colours were red, black and yellow. In those days players often wore different caps and Murdoch might well have worn this one again on the 1884 tour. On available evidence it is the oldest Australian Test cap in existence.

Photo: courtesy Keith Hayhurst

Top shelf … wearing this cap in South Africa in 1949-50 Keith Miller scored 246 runs at 41.00 batting at number three and captured 17 wickets at 22.94 in another consummate all-round performance.

Photo: Legends Genuine Memorabilia

Immortal … the cap worn by the legendary Victor Trumper when he made his Test debut at the age of 21 in England at the close of the 19th century. As his legend grew this cap spawned the iconic baggy green, the symbol of Australian cricket in the 21st century.

Photo: Legends Genuine Memorabilia

Number one … a baggy green belonging to Don Bradman is the most valuable item of memorabilia for collectors and museums, and his 1948 cap the most valuable of all. Here a young Bradman wears his 1931-32 Test cap.

Photo: courtesy Bradman Museum

Variations on a theme ... (clockwise from top left) Victor Trumper's baggy green for the tour to England in 1909, Edgar Mayne's cap for the triangular series with South Africa in England in 1912, Bill Hunt's baggy for the home series with South Africa in 1931-32, and Don Bradman's cap for the Ashes series in 1936-37.

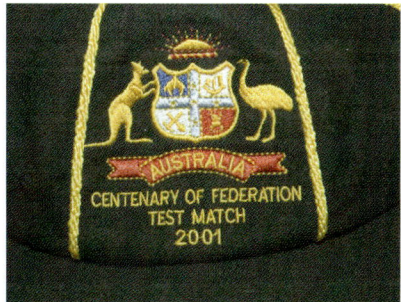

Capital idea ... caps created for the Bicentennial Test played at the SCG from January 29, 1988 and for the Centenary of Federation Test played at the SCG from January 2, 2001.

Photo: Legends Genuine Memorabilia

Value added ... a collection of Australian Test caps from various eras. Clockwise from bottom left: a 1949-50 cap, a women's baggy green, one of the mini caps given to former Test players at a reunion in 2003, and a current baggy green. Centre: the numbered cap bag given to Phil Jaques in 2006-07.

Photo: courtesy of Albion C&D